THE OPEN
CHAMPIONSHIP
2001

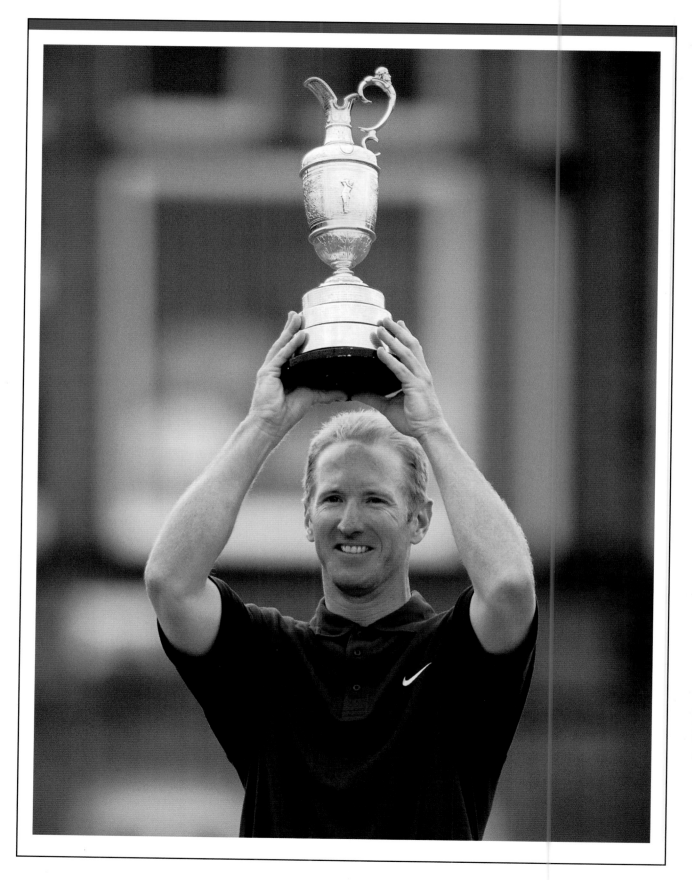

130TH OPEN CHAMPIONSHIP
Card of the Championship Course

Hole	Par	Yards	Hole	Par	Yards
1	3	206	10	4	335
2	4	438	11	5	542
3	4	458	12	3	198
4	4	392	13	4	342
5	3	212	14	4	445
6	5	494	15	4	465
7	5	557	16	4	359
8	4	419	17	4	467
9	3	164	18	4	412
Out	35	3,340	In	36	3,565
			Total	71	6,905

Railway

THE OPEN CHAMPIONSHIP 2001

WRITERS
ROBERT SOMMERS
MICHAEL MCDONNELL
MARINO PARASCENZO
ANDY FARRELL
RON SIRAK
JOHN HOPKINS

PHOTOGRAPHERS
MICHAEL COHEN
PHIL INGLIS

EDITOR
BEV NORWOOD

www.opengolf.com

AUTHORISED BY THE
CHAMPIONSHIP COMMITTEE
OF THE ROYAL AND ANCIENT
GOLF CLUB OF ST ANDREWS

HAZLETON PUBLISHING LTD
3 Richmond Hill, Richmond, Surrey TW10 6RE

Published 2001 by Hazleton Publishing Ltd
Copyright © 2001 The Championship Committee Merchandising
Limited

Statistics of 130th Open Championship produced on a
Unisys Computer System

Photographs on pages 10-11, 14-16 courtesy of Stephen Szurlej.
Photograph on page 17 courtesy of Fred Vuich.

A CIP catalogue record for this book is available
from the British Library

ISBN: 1-903135-04-4

Type and layout by Davis Design
Printed in Great Britain
by Butler & Tanner, Frome, Somerset

CONTENTS

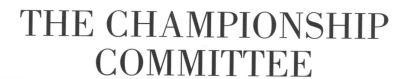

THE CHAMPIONSHIP COMMITTEE

CHAIRMAN

H. M. CAMPBELL

DEPUTY CHAIRMAN

D. I. PEPPER

COMMITTEE

M. C. GRINT
J. R. JONES
J. M. KIPPAX
G. C. MARKS
P. D. MONTGOMERY
D. K. RAE
M. C. TATE
M. YATES

ADDITIONAL MEMBER

W. G. BLACK
COUNCIL OF NATIONAL GOLF UNIONS

SECRETARY

P. DAWSON

CHAMPIONSHIP SECRETARY

D. HILL

RULES SECRETARY

D. E. RICKMAN

INTRODUCTION

BY H. M. CAMPBELL

Chairman of Championship Committee
The Royal and Ancient Golf Club of St Andrews

For the sixth time in the last seven years an American won the Open Championship. This time David Duval, with rounds of 65 and 67 on Saturday and Sunday, came through the field to win by three shots with a 72-hole total of 274 and secure his first major championship success.

The St Andrews Open in the year 2000 was always going to be difficult to follow, but the 130th Open at Royal Lytham and St Annes managed to do so in some style.

In spite of a dreadfully wet winter and spring, Paul Smith and his greenkeeping team presented the course in magnificent condition, and in spite of rather calm conditions, the players were well tested by the natural challenges of this fine links course.

Once more a record crowd at Lytham were entertained by some fine golf which produced a hole-in-one, two albatrosses, many eagles, and over 1200 birdies during the week.

Over 2200 competitors entered the Championship and the Royal and Ancient Golf Club Championship Committee are very grateful to the 16 regional and four final qualifying courses that helped us to reduce the original entry to the starting field of 156.

The Captain, Committee, and members of the host club provided enthusiastic support both before and during the championship and their efforts were greatly appreciated by our Championship Committee.

Finally I would like to thank the photographers and writers whose contribution has helped to record a memorable Open in the following pages.

H. M. Campbell

FOREWORD
BY DAVID DUVAL

It has been a wonderful experience to compete in the Open Championship. Now that I have become champion I am thrilled to be part of the long history of the tournament. I can hold the claret jug, recognise all the names on it and see my name there too. That is a tremendous honour.

When I was growing up in Florida, the Open came on television early in the mornings, and I remember watching and realising how different golf was here from the golf that I was playing. I saw how the courses looked different and the atmosphere was different, with the dust and grass flying, and how you never had anyone trying to carry shots over lakes as we did at home. It was so different to what I was used to playing, and I looked forward to when I could come over here myself.

I was lucky to experience my first Open in 1995 at St Andrews. I got a taste of Scottish golf the week before at Carnoustie and I loved it. I have enjoyed coming back every year since then.

Royal Lytham and St Annes was a very difficult test, but I came to recognise that we are just playing a game and maybe that's some of the reason I felt so good this week. It's only when you are done that you look back and you realise how much you have enjoyed the challenge, how much you have enjoyed playing. I came away with many great memories and a sense of accomplishment that I will never forget.

David Duval

The final hole at Royal Lytham and St Annes provides a classic finish with a landing area flanked by bunkers.

ROUND ROYAL LYTHAM & ST ANNES

No 1 206 Yards, Par 3

No gentle introduction this, but ample warning of the demands that lie ahead. The tee shot is played through an avenue of trees to a green protected by severe bunkers, with the out-of-bounds railway line flanking the right-hand side.

No 2 438 Yards, Par 4

The out-of-bounds railway line still flanks the right-hand side, even though the ideal tee shot should favour that side to open up the green, which sits at an angle and slopes from left to right. The timid tee shot could be snared by bunkers on the left side.

No 3 458 Yards, Par 4

The longest par-4 hole on the first nine requires two sturdy but well-directed shots, with a tee shot that must avoid the left bunkers but not drift too far on the cross-wind. The approach must climb to a raised green and avoid bunkers either side.

No 4 392 Yards, Par 4

This hole turns back in the opposite direction and is a left-hand dogleg that favours a tee shot placed wide enough to see the green that is heavily bunkered. If the ball is positioned too far left, there is virtually no sight of the target for the approach.

No 5 212 Yards, Par 3

The longest of the par-3s demands an arrow-straight tee shot to avoid the bunkers that cluster round the green. Moreover, there is a stretch of "dead ground" in front of the green that is deceptive and makes the hole play longer than it appears.

No 6 494 Yards, Par 5

A birdie chance, but only if the tee shot finds an accommodating lie to provide a clear route over the cross bunkers to a slightly crowned green guarded by bunkers on either side. The best line from the tee favours the right side of the fairway.

No 7 557 Yards, Par 5

This is the longest hole, which follows a gentle right-hand dogleg route. The prospect of a birdie must be balanced against the perils with heavy bunkering on both sides of the fairways, particularly closest to the green, which is slightly sunken.

No 8 419 Yards, Par 4

The right-hand railway comes back into play again and presents a real threat for any shot that drifts away from the elevated and therefore exposed tee. The prudent selection is a long iron and then an equally crucial choice for the approach to the plateau green that is protected by a range of cross bunkers 40 yards from the putting surface.

No 9 164 Yards, Par 3

Even though this is the shortest hole on the course, the demand for precision is vital because of the nine bunkers that protect the green on all sides and add to the pressures of finding the right area from which to make a reasonable birdie attempt.

No 10 335 Yards, Par 4

The start of a long journey home, particularly if the wind has been favourable on the way out. The tee shot is blind to an angled fairway and therefore demands a sound memory to find the right position from which to attack a rather small green.

No 11 542 Yards, Par 5

Decision time for the big hitters as to whether they take the left-hand route to clear the cross bunkers for a shorter and more direct line to the green. The risks are huge, because the rough is ruinous and the intended landing area extremely narrow.

No 12 198 Yards, Par 3

The most difficult of all the short holes because there is out of bounds close to the right edge of the green, which itself is raised and angled. The prevailing wind comes from the left, so that the tee shot must be held up against it.

No 13 342 Yards, Par 4

The gentle start to Murder Mile—six successive par-4s measuring well over 2,000 yards that assuredly determine the difference between a good or a bad score. It is the last chance of a safe birdie before the hard work begins.

No 14 445 Yards, Par 4

The tee shot has to avoid the bunkers and sand hills on the right to provide a reasonable approach to the green, so the margin for error is minimal, particularly with rough and out of bounds so close to the right side of the putting surface.

No 15 465 Yards, Par 4

New bunkers have been added to the existing problems of cutting the corner of the fairway to bring the green within range. The approach has to find its way between dunes and cross bunkers with rough to the left and sand traps to the right.

No 16 359 Yards, Par 4

The tee shot is blind, but still needs to be well placed to provide a trouble-free route to the green, unlike the effort of Seve Ballesteros, who played his approach from an overflow car park on the right after an errant drive yet still emerged with a birdie on his way to winning in 1979.

No 17 467 Yards, Par 4

The landing area from the tee is claustrophobically small between a range of bunkers on the left and dense scrub and bushes to the right. The hole turns left towards an open green protected by bunkers on either side.

No 18 412 Yards, Par 4

The classic finish with a landing area flanked by bunkers and the added menace of cross bunkers in the fairway. The brave drive is rewarded with a gentler approach that still needs to be treated with respect, because Royal Lytham remains a test of skill until the final stroke.

WHERE NO ONE ESCAPES

BY MICHAEL MCDONNELL

Even a cursory study of the landscape over which Royal Lytham and St Annes extends reveals a glaring truth that the punishment for error rarely fits the crime but more frequently is mercilessly out of proportion to it.

What might seem to be the most trivial and fractional aberration in judgement or execution is met with a degree of harshness that rightfully gives the Lancashire course its awesome reputation as one of the most exhaustive examinations in championship golf, with unquestionably the most gruelling finishing stretch of five holes lying in wait to ambush both hope and ambition.

Of course, such arbitrary and random sanctions observe the fundamental requirement of links golf, and probably the game itself, in that it must stand as a test of character and patience as much as a challenge of required playing skills. But these constant dangers also dictate a choice of strategies available to each campaigner on how best to cope, and in turn depend wholly on individual temperament.

When Peter Thomson defeated David Thomas in a 36-hole play-off for the 1958 Open title, he followed a cleverly calculated, stepping-stone attack in which he played to specific safety zones on every fairway that took the hazards out of play and allowed him a safe route to the green.

Then, too, in 1974 Gary Player—not the longest striker of his day—virtually abandoned the driver for his one iron from the tee for the sole purpose of keeping the ball in play on the fairways and away from the ruinous hazards and rough that seemed to menace almost every shot.

Alternatively, however, there is the full-frontal, no-holds-barred, devil-may-care approach in which the course and its perils are tackled head-on in the steadfast and fatalistic belief that if the gods have decreed it is your turn to win then no amount of disaster or set-back will prevent you.

Seve Ballesteros called it "destino" and he should know, having twice triumphed at Royal Lytham and St Annes by carving a route that at times bore little resemblance to the plan originally laid out on the present site by George Low in 1897 and retouched here and there down the years by such distinguished architects as Harry Colt, Herbert Fowler, and C.K. Cotton.

The car park beside the 16th fairway from which Ballesteros played a spectacular approach shot in winning the 1979 title was a case in point. But there were other moments, too, that prompted runner-up Hale Irwin to mutter in baffled tones, "I can't understand how anyone can drive that badly and still win an Open Championship."

It was a helter-skelter ride for both Ballesteros and his fans, and as thrilling and nerve-racking as any funfair offering to be found up the road at the pleasure beach in Blackpool. The late Peter Dobereiner summed up the mood beautifully in *The Guardian* the next day.

"The dust of that brutal assault has not yet settled," he wrote. "Debris will continue to fall. It will take awhile for the spectators of the violence to recover; we are dazed like witnesses to a nearby explosion ... not a scratch on us, but the medics know we are candidates for a cup of sweet, strong tea and a quiet lie-down. Tranquillity will come later."

Not that Ballesteros was the first campaigner at Royal Lytham to put complete faith in the maxim that fortune favours the brave, because in 1969 Tony Jacklin adopted a similar attitude as he became the first home player for 18 years to win the championship. His final round stands as a masterpiece of composure and tempo, but there had been earlier struggles to keep his game under control and himself in contention.

J.L. Manning, the distinguished columnist for the *Daily Mail* at the time, followed Jacklin through the

The 458-yard third is the longest par-4 hole on the first nine and requires two sturdy, well directed shots.

third round and outlined the young man's travails the next day to his readers: "There was punishment all the way. He was the boxer who had been knocked down but refused to go out. The champion in the making got his ball everywhere except on the fairway, playing those last four holes. It was not good golf. But it was one hell of a fight."

The truth is that nobody—not even the winners—ever escape from Royal Lytham unscathed. It was here in 1963 that Jack Nicklaus made what he called in his autobiography "the biggest mental blunders of my career," which cost him his chance of the title or at least a place in the play-off.

As he stood on the 18th tee, Nicklaus assumed incorrectly that he held a two-stroke lead over Bob Charles and Phil Rodgers, who were playing behind him. In fact, they had cut his lead to one stroke and then drew level with birdies on the 16th. Nicklaus in reality needed to par the last hole to have any chance of a play-off, but drove into a bunker and finished with a bogey 5.

Nicklaus recalled in his book: "By the time Bob made history the next day in the last of the British Open's 36-hole play-offs by becoming the first left-hander to win a major championship, I was well on my way to Dallas, Texas, for the PGA Champion-

ship. It would be extremely hot in Dallas, but not as hot as I was for most of that five-thousand-mile aeroplane ride."

So confident had Nicklaus been of victory that day that he was convinced his name would be on the trophy by the end of it and reflected, "I'm not a gambler, but if I had been, I would have bet a tidy sum as the final round began at Royal Lytham and St Annes that, at its end, the letters flowing from the engraver's needle would end up spelling Jack Nicklaus."

But then this closing stretch is both dangerous and damaging, as Gary Player found in 1974 when he conducted a frantic search for his ball in long grass behind the 17th green before dropping a stroke, then playing left-handed with the back of his putter from the side of the clubhouse for another bogey on the last hole after his ball ran through the green.

It says much for the domination he held in that championship, the first in which the 1.68-inch diameter "big ball" was made compulsory, that these blemishes had no significant effect on the outcome. He still finished four strokes clear of his nearest challenger, Peter Oosterhuis, to become Open champion for the third time in his career.

Even Bobby Jones was confronted by a sickening

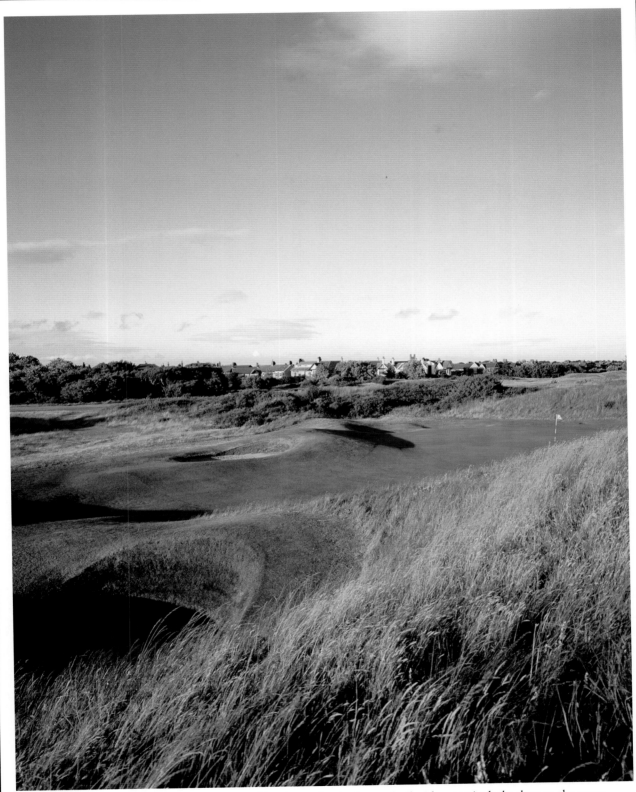

The seventh is the longest hole, 557 yards, and has heavy bunkering on both sides, particularly close to the green.

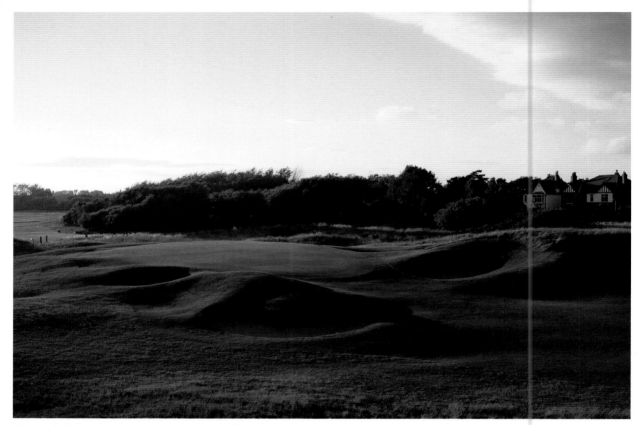

The 10th hole offers a tee shot that is blind to an angled fairway and then a small green.

crisis back in 1926 when he was tied for the lead with playing partner Al Watrous, the American professional, as they tackled the 17th. It was in fact the second drama of that day, because at lunch time he and Watrous had gone back to their hotel before the start of the final round, but were then refused re-admission to the course because they had forgotten their badges. Jones handled the crisis perfectly by buying a couple of tickets to get in.

He showed similar coolness under pressure when it looked as though Watrous had taken the advantage by hitting the green with his second shot while Jones was trapped in a sandy waste 175 yards away from a green he could not see. He chose a four iron and described the predicament graphically in his 1927 autobiography: "… an eighth of an inch too deep with your blade, off dry sand, and the shot expires in front of your eyes. And if your blade is a thought too high—I will dismiss this harrowing reflection."

In fact, the ball was taken cleanly and carried majestically to the green, then spun obediently to a halt closer to the hole than Watrous, who seemed to sense what was about to happen and murmured "there goes a hundred thousand bucks" as he saw his chance of becoming champion vanish.

Even so, Jones had to wait anxiously in the long room overlooking that last green to find out whether Walter Hagen, still prowling out on the course, could snatch the title from him. O.B. Keeler, the Atlanta sports columnist and close friend of Jones, wrote in glowing fashion at the time: "The plot was complete; two great golfers in a death grip—and behind them the Old Haig, set to knock them both off."

But it never quite happened and Hagen came to the 18th needing to hole his second shot to tie. He even sent his caddie forward to attend the flagstick, but the ball ran through and cost him a 6 for a share of third place.

In fact, American golfers occupied the top four places and prompted a caustic comment from Arthur Leonard Lee, then golf writer for the *Manchester Guardian*. "Truly the British rout is complete," he wrote. "We shall have to reconcile ourselves to the ignominious position of arranging competitions for Americans to win."

In a sense that final drama between Jones and Watrous had been the stuff of pure match play, and it is an intriguing fact that Royal Lytham and St

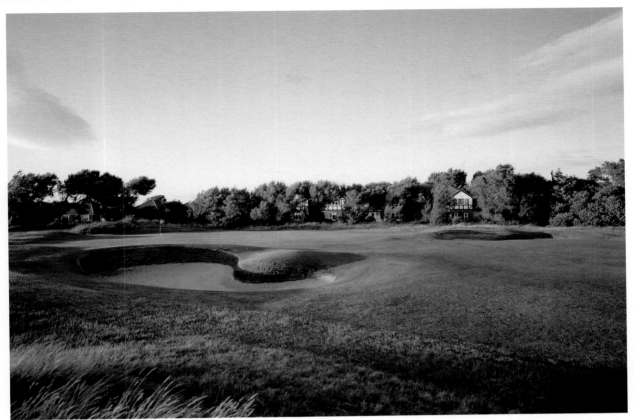

The margin for error is minimal on the 14th, with bunkers protecting the green and with rough and out of bounds right.

Annes has a proud and distinguished record as the arena in which many such classic head-to-head encounters have taken place in two Ryder Cup matches as well as a Curtis Cup and numerous amateur championships.

Nick Faldo won the English amateur title there in 1975 and two years later returned as a fully fledged professional to win his singles match against Tom Watson in the Ryder Cup. Peter Alliss engaged in an unforgettable scrap with Arnold Palmer in the 1961 Ryder Cup in which both men sportingly conceded the other's putt on the final green for a halved match. It was a gesture that held more than just mutual respect, because these gladiators had battled at close quarters to breathtaking levels of performance and then seemed to sense it would have been wrong for either of them to lose over a trivial putt.

All of which prompts an obvious curiosity about the inherent qualities of the Lancashire course and how they have combined or coincided to make it such an ideal examination that extends beyond a dogmatic insistence to stay steady and straight and allow opponents to take the risks. Perhaps the truth is that Royal Lytham, of all the championship courses, still offers in greater measure the vagaries and vicissitudes of links golf as an integral—indeed essential—part of the test to determine the champion. Slide rule golf is not enough. Invention, ingenuity and imagination were among the original talents of the royal and ancient game, and they are still relevant at Royal Lytham.

Invariably the process of winning any championship begins without fuss or attention, then builds to a climax until the supreme moment is reached. Through it all, the new champion has endured a campaign mixed with misfortune and good fortune, but somehow found a way that others could not follow. In the aftermath of such triumph, an intriguing affinity begins between the champion and the course. It is possession without ownership, based on memories that will remain with him for the rest of his life.

Tony Jacklin, the 1969 champion, defined that special affinity between a winner and his field of play when, long past his glory days, he still made the pilgrimage back to Royal Lytham and St Annes for the Open Championship. He said quite simply, "Lytham will always be my course. So here I am, ploughing on."

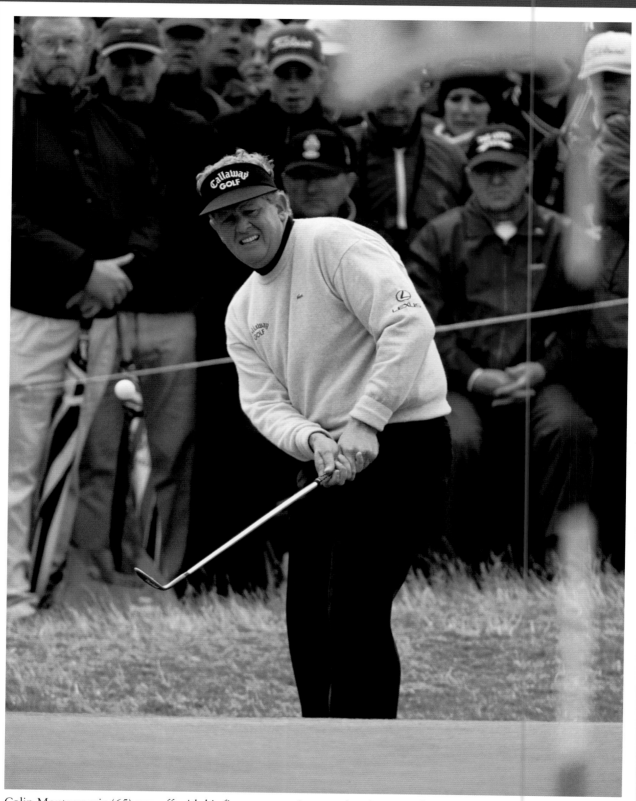

Colin Montgomerie (65) was off with his first-ever opening round under 70 in the Open Championship.

A GOOD START, FINALLY

BY ROBERT SOMMERS

It had taken awhile. It had taken years of frustration and failure, years of doubt and dejection, of anxiety and stress, of unending pressure and tension, but on a cool, overcast morning at Royal Lytham and St Annes, Colin Montgomerie finally began an Open Championship playing the kind of golf everyone knew he could play. Loping along in his recognisable long strides while an enthusiastic gallery cheered every step, Montgomerie tore through Royal Lytham's first nine in 30 strokes, came back in 35, shot 65, and for all anyone knew, had taken the 130th Open Championship by the throat. If someone else wanted it, he would have to tear it from Montgomerie's hands.

This exceptional round turned Montgomerie into a hero. With every birdie, galleries that had not always been kind to him now willed him on, calling encouragement, applauding, and racing after him, jostling for a good spot to watch. Reacting to their spirit, Montgomerie wiped away his usual intense expression and replaced it with a mile-wide grin that grew with every cheer.

When a 40-foot putt dropped at the 18th, the thought occurred that Montgomerie might have wished his day had never ended. But Montgomerie was a realist. Knowing this might not go on very long, he said later, "Let's hope they'll be cheering as much the rest of the week."

The final putt climaxed a peculiar day. There was Montgomerie, who had never played very well in the Open, leading the field by three strokes, and there was Tiger Woods, at par 71, tied for 34th place, and Retief Goosen, the US Open champion, much farther back, tied for 87th place with 74.

Actually, with the 156-man field so tightly bunched, and with three more rounds to play, hardly anyone could be considered out of contention.

Montgomerie stood three strokes ahead of Brad Faxon, Chris DiMarco, and Mikko Ilonen, a former Amateur champion. The next 46 players, though, were camped within two strokes of one another, and they included much of the game's upper echelon.

David Duval, Jose Maria Olazabal, and Jesper Parnevik opened with 69, Mark O'Meara, Darren Clarke, Phil Mickelson, Vijay Singh, and Sergio Garcia shot 70, and Ernie Els and Woods were amongst the 18 men tied at 71.

Altogether, 33 men broke par, 18 matched it, and 35 more shot within two strokes of par. Excluding Montgomerie, 85 players were within five strokes of one another. At one time during the day, 52 players had worked their way to two under par, and 20 of them had gone three under.

Jeff Maggert dropped to four under par briefly by holing a full-blooded six iron for an albatross 2 on the sixth, but he lost five strokes over the remaining 12 holes, shot 40 on the second nine, and 72 for the round.

Amongst the old heroes, Sandy Lyle, the 1985 champion, battled his way to three under par twice, but he, too, lost it all and shot 72, one over par.

Others did worse. Playing his usual erratic golf, Mickelson got to two under par through the 13th with only three par holes. He birdied the second, bogeyed the next three, then scored consecutive eagle 3s on the sixth and seventh. From there on he struggled to hold what he had wrung from Royal Lytham, but ended up giving one of those strokes away.

Paired with Montgomerie, Fred Couples was amongst those who got to three under par, but he lost every one of those strokes on the 14th. With his approach buried under the lip of a greenside bunker, Couples flailed at his ball four times to hack it onto the green, one of the shots left-handed, made 7, and fell to level par.

Even so, Couples did better than Jim Furyk. Two under par after the 10th, Furyk ran into all kinds of trouble on the 11th, the last of Lytham's par-5s. His

Brad Faxon (68) shared second place at three under par despite posting four bogeys.

Mikko Ilonen (68) was the 2000 Amateur champion.

drive settled into an unplayable lie in the rough, his approach caught the top of a bunker and fell in, and his recovery caromed off the bunker's face and hit him, costing him still two more penalty strokes. When he finally holed out he had taken 10 strokes and gone from two under par to three over. Shaken, he lost three more strokes coming in, played the second nine in 43, shot 77 and had lost all hope of making the 36-hole cut.

Losing strokes almost as quickly, Nick Faldo, three under after seven, took a 6 on the eighth, a par-4, a 4 on the ninth, a 5 on the 10th, and a 6 on the 11th. He had five strokes gone in four holes. Out in 35, he came back in 40 and shot 75. Goosen, the winner of two national championships within the last month, worked his way to two under through 13 holes, bogeyed the next three, double-bogeyed the next, and shot 74.

Those were disappointing rounds, to be sure, but they didn't carry the impact of the loose play by Woods, who had established himself as the best player of his time. At 25 he had already won six times in the game's four major championships, and while he had played some shoddy stuff in the US Open a month earlier, it didn't seem likely he would repeat.

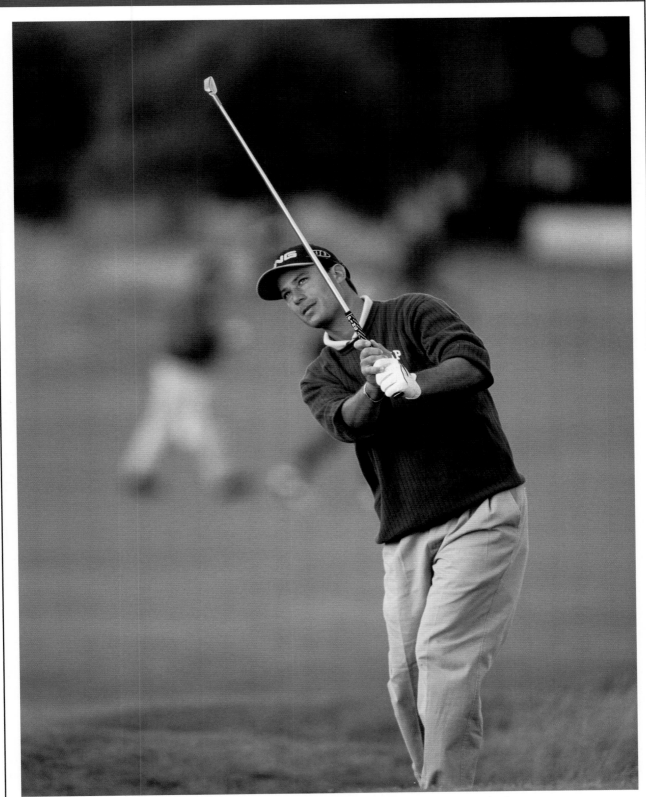

Chris DiMarco (68) recovered from a bogey on the first hole and a double bogey on the third.

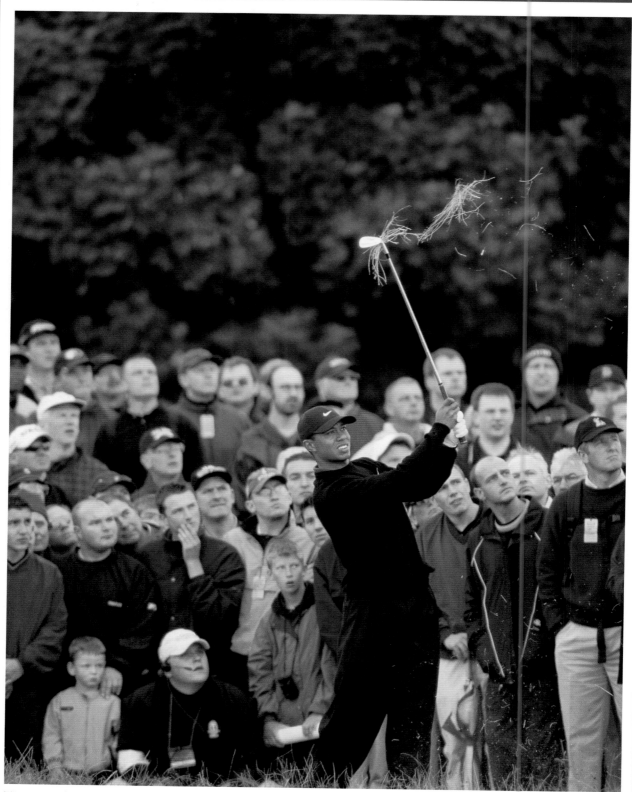

Tiger Woods (71) was not hitting the ball as he would have liked, yet he managed to finish at level par.

When he played his first stroke, at nine o'clock Thursday morning, he looked as if he might run away with this Open, just as he had at St Andrews a year earlier. Unique amongst courses where the great championships are played, Royal Lytham opens with a testing par-3 of 206 yards that begins in a protected chute, then opens to the wind and runs to a green guarded by bunkers.

With a 10-mile-an-hour breeze at his back, Woods floated a seven iron that landed softly and pulled up within 15 feet of the hole. Of course he ran the putt home, and with a birdie 2 looked for all the world to be off on one of the great rounds. Another stunning pitch to the second left him with half the distance of the first putt, but his ball refused to fall. So sure had he been of his line, that when the ball slipped past the hole, Woods looked stunned. Worse was coming.

From a good drive in the fairway, he left his approach to the third short and right of the green, but he still salvaged a par, then played the kind of shot that had tormented him throughout the US Open. With an iron in his hand and his ball sitting on a peg, he flew his drive off to the right towards tall and wispy grass bordering the fourth fairway. It missed the grass and instead burrowed into a deep pot bunker at the base of a high knob.

This was quite a strange experience. A year earlier at St Andrews, Woods had never once hit a ball into a bunker—72 holes without playing a shot from sand. Now, with the bunker's sheer walls, buttressed by sod, rising sharply, Woods sacrificed a shot and pitched back to the fairway. Now he must have sensed that his game was still off-colour. When he saw his approach flying towards the green's back left corner, miles from the hole, he flipped his club to his caddie and walked away, apparently disgusted. He bogeyed and was back to level par.

Next he overshot the green of the fifth, a 212-yard par-3, but saved his par, then moved on to the sixth, the shortest and easiest of Lytham's par-5 holes. Here Woods pulled his drive into the left rough and chopped it out into another deep bunker set in front of the green. Instead of a birdie 4 on an eminently reachable par-5, he parred. It was a chance gone.

The seventh was another par-5, vulnerable to the

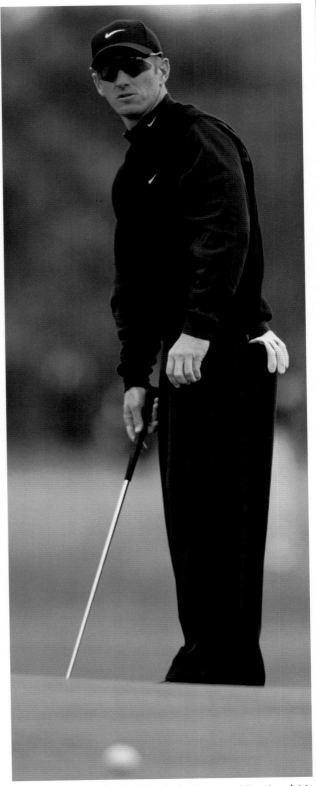

David Duval (69) birdied five holes between Nos 6 and 11.

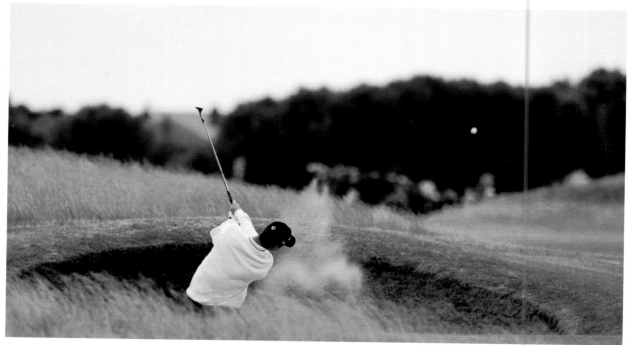

Justin Rose (69) felt his play to start the Open was a continuation of his good year.

Paul McGinley (69) recorded six birdies.

biggest hitters. Once again Woods missed a fairway and parred a hole he should birdie at least half the time.

On and on it went. He made another bogey at the ordinarily easy 10th, a short par-4 of just 335 yards, and when he bogeyed the 14th, his third of the day, he had matched his total of all 72 holes of the 2000 Open.

Woods closed out his day with another scrambling par at the 18th, driving into the rough once again, pitching into another greenside bunker and saving the 4. He was in with 71.

His had been a loose sort of round, not the kind of golf he had shown in that remarkable run through the US Open, the Open, and the USPGA Championship in 2000, then the Masters in April of 2001. In both the US Open and the first round of the Open, he had driven into unfamiliar places, missed greens, and the putts that had usually fallen grazed the lips of the holes, looked in, and turned away.

At the same time, he had mis-played shots into five bunkers, nearly as many as he had hit fairways and greens. He had hit only eight fairways at Lytham and nine greens, and while some putts that might have fallen slipped past, he one-putted half the greens— six of them to save par.

Perhaps even more significantly, Woods did not birdie even one of the three fairly easy par-5 holes. The sixth measured just 494 yards, the seventh 557 yards, and the 11th 542 yards. In the age of drivers

Jose Maria Olazabal (69) said iron play was the "key factor" in his round.

with metal heads and balls with aerodynamically correct dimple patterns and exotic compositions stuffed inside, holes of these lengths fall within the range of second shots. Even the 642-yard fifth hole at Southern Hills, the site of the US Open a month earlier, was reached several times with second shots.

His wasn't a fatal round, though. Through all his loose golf, scrambling to make pars where they had come so easily in the past, missing opportunities to pick up strokes, Woods had done what the great players usually do—he turned in a decent score even though he had not played his best. At day's end Montgomerie would lead him by just six strokes with 54 holes to play, and as Monty himself pointed out, he was only three strokes out of second place. No one ahead of him could sleep easily.

Early in the day, the usual vast gallery had lined up waiting for Woods to start, jamming the grandstand behind the first green and lining up four- and five-deep along the fairway ropes. They romped along with him through the early holes, but when word spread that Montgomerie was off on a tear, they began drifting away to chase after him. Only a few left at first, but as Montgomerie piled up the birdies and Woods struggled, more and more left, searching for more excitement.

They certainly found it with Montgomerie, especially through the heart-thumping second nine.

Montgomerie had always been a puzzle, a player

Stuart Appleby (69) finished with a birdie on the 17th.

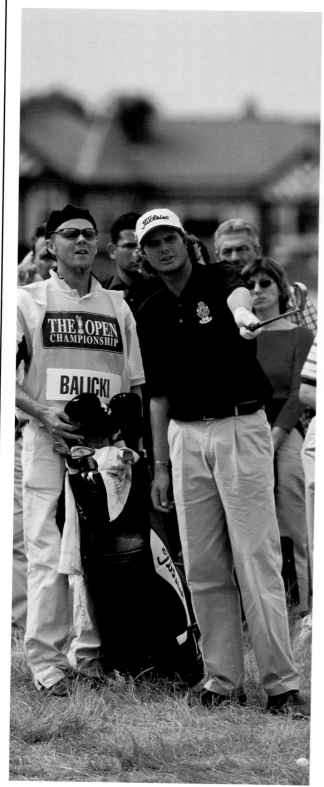

Alexandre Balicki (69) started well in his first Open.

Billy Mayfair (69) had three birdies in his first nine.

with enormous ability but one who had yet to win one of the four most important championships. He had come close to winning three US Opens and one USPGA Championship, but someone else always played better.

Locked in a tie for 25th place, he played a superb closing round of 70 in high winds at Pebble Beach in the 1992 US Open. For a short time it looked as if his 288 might win, but then both Tom Kite and Jeff Sluman played better, and Montgomerie dropped to third place.

Twice more he nearly won a US Open, but he lost both of them to Ernie Els, first in a play-off at Oakmont in 1994, then at Congressional in 1997.

He lost another play-off to Steve Elkington in the 1995 USPGA Championship, but he had never come close to winning the Masters.

These losses hurt, certainly, but nothing matched the pain of his failures in the Open Championship. Not only had he not won, for the most part he had played badly. Coming to Royal Lytham and St Annes, Montgomerie had played 11 Opens and only once finished within sight of the leader. Shooting 275 at Turnberry in 1994, he tied for eighth, seven strokes behind Nick Price.

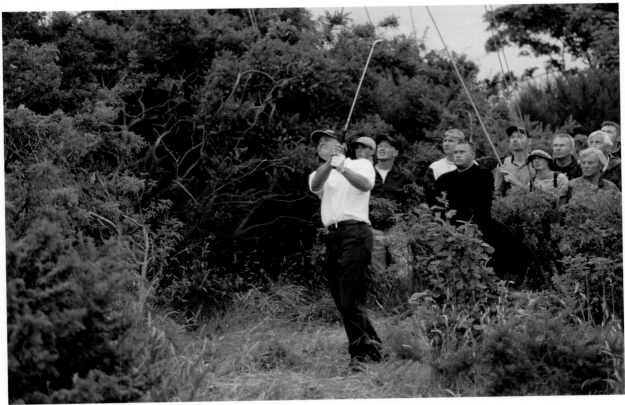

Niclas Fasth (69) scrambled here on the 18th hole but still posted a birdie.

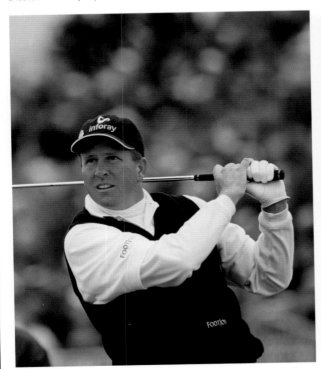

J.P. Hayes (69) was in his first Open start.

Miguel Angel Jimenez (69) was two over par after four.

Sergio Garcia (70) had two wins this year.

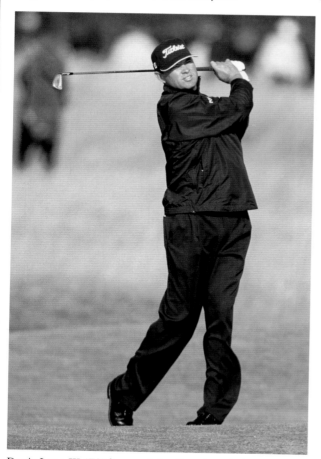

Davis Love III (73) bogeyed the first three holes.

Worse, in five of the previous nine Opens, he hadn't even qualified to play the last two rounds.

It was hardly a wonder, then, that when Montgomerie led off with a barrage of birdies, the galleries flocked to him. He did not disappoint them.

Because he played third in his starting time, Montgomerie had a good break on the first hole. When the six irons of both Fred Couples and Stuart Appleby fell short, Montgomerie switched to a five iron, hit the green, and rolled in a putt from about 20 feet. Quickly, then, he added another birdie at the second, holing from no more than six feet. He was two under after two holes.

One stroke was gone when his four iron missed the fifth green, but he chipped into the hole of the sixth for an eagle 3, then played a couple of gorgeous irons, to 10 feet on the eighth and about five feet on the ninth, holed both putts, and began the homeward nine five under par.

By now the gallery cheered every step and Montgomerie savoured the support. He had shot low rounds in important championships before, but he had never gone out in 30. Now he would have to hold his concentration and not let a great round slip away.

He added another birdie on the 10th, where a 30-footer fell. Six under par after 10 holes, he was just one stroke away from the course record of 64 Tom Lehman had set in 1996.

There was no birdie on the 11th, but a battle to save par instead, then another on the dangerous 12th, a vicious par-3 of 198 yards. He made a routine 4 on the 13th, then a slip on the 14th, where he might have been distracted by Couples' struggles with the bunker. Montgomerie took three putts and bogeyed. He was five under now with Lytham's severe finishing holes still ahead.

The gallery had grown with every hole, and now they rushed after him, calling his name and willing him on to a strong finish.

Those last few holes turned into a struggle. He had missed only three greens through the first 14 holes, but now he missed three consecutively. Still he made his figures, holing from 20 feet on the 15th and from inside 10 feet on the 16th and 17th. Then he cli-

Phil Mickelson (70) had eagle 3s on the sixth and seventh.

Vijay Singh (70) was level on the par-5 holes.

maxed his round by birdieing the 18th from 40 feet. When the putt dropped, the roar rising from the home hole's giant grandstands must have startled the crowds throughout the golf course.

Montgomerie had shot 65s before—at Oakmont in the second round of the 1994 US Open, at Congressional in the first round of the 1997 US Open, at Riviera in the last round of the 1995 USPGA Championship, and even at Turnberry in the third round of the 1994 Open—but he had never begun an Open with such sparkling golf. He had, in fact, never scored lower than 71.

On this day, though, he played as he had seldom played in the past. Accurate as usual, he put his ball in 11 of the 14 fairways on driving holes, and he hit 12 greens, which under the tension of an Open is pretty good. Then he holed everything he looked at —just 24 putts in all, a performance that was hurt by his lapse on the 14th.

But this was just the first round, and Montgomerie knew it very well. With so many of his followers ready to concede him the championship, Montgomerie reminded everyone just what this day amounted to.

"All this is is a good start," he cautioned. "It's the best start I've ever made in an Open, and it's nice to at last be in contention here, but there is an awfully long way to go. I will start out tomorrow as if nothing has happened. I will have to go out and play the way I did today. The one thing I must not do is defend."

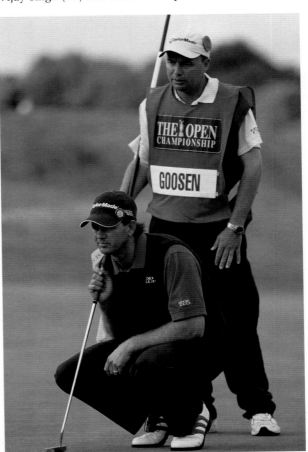

Retief Goosen (74) had just won at Loch Lomond.

Towering above the Open Championship were the cranes topped with television cameras.

FIRST ROUND RESULTS

HOLE	1	2	3	4	5	6	7	8	9	10	11	12	13	14	15	16	17	18	TOTAL
PAR	3	4	4	4	3	5	5	4	3	4	5	3	4	4	4	4	4	4	TOTAL
Colin Montgomerie	2	3	4	4	4	3	5	3	2	3	5	3	4	5	4	4	4	3	65
Brad Faxon	3	3	5	4	3	3	4	3	4	4	4	4	4	4	4	4	3	5	68
Chris DiMarco	4	3	6	4	3	4	4	4	2	4	4	3	3	4	4	5	3	4	68
Mikko Ilonen	2	4	3	4	3	5	5	4	2	4	5	3	3	5	4	4	4	4	68
Justin Rose	3	4	4	4	3	5	3	4	3	4	4	3	3	4	5	4	4	4	69
Miguel Angel Jimenez	3	4	5	5	3	4	4	5	3	4	4	3	3	5	5	3	4	4	69
Paul McGinley	2	4	5	4	3	4	4	5	2	4	4	4	4	4	5	4	4	3	69
J.P. Hayes	3	3	4	4	4	4	4	5	2	3	4	3	4	5	4	4	4	4	69
David Duval	3	4	4	5	4	4	4	4	2	3	4	3	4	4	5	4	4	4	69
Jose Maria Olazabal	3	3	4	4	3	4	5	3	3	4	4	4	4	4	5	4	4	4	69
Stuart Appleby	3	4	4	4	4	4	5	2	4	6	3	4	4	4	4	4	3	4	69
Pierre Fulke	3	4	4	4	2	4	5	3	3	4	4	3	5	4	4	4	5	4	69
Billy Andrade	3	5	4	4	3	5	5	3	3	3	5	3	4	3	4	4	4	4	69
Alexandre Balicki	3	4	4	4	3	4	5	4	3	3	5	3	5	4	3	4	4	3	69
Niclas Fasth	3	4	4	4	4	4	5	3	4	4	4	5	4	5	4	4	3		69
Alex Cejka	3	4	4	4	2	4	6	4	3	4	4	3	4	5	3	4	4		69
Jesper Parnevik	3	4	4	5	2	3	4	4	4	4	5	4	3	4	5	3	4	4	69
Billy Mayfair	3	4	5	3	3	4	4	4	3	4	4	4	4	4	4	4	4		69
Greg Owen	3	4	4	3	3	5	4	5	3	4	4	3	4	4	4	5	4	4	69
Joe Ogilvie	4	4	4	3	3	4	5	3	3	4	4	3	4	4	4	5	4	4	69

HOLE SUMMARY

HOLE	PAR	EAGLES	BIRDIES	PARS	BOGEYS	D. BOGEYS	HIGHER	RANK	AVERAGE
1	3	0	8	121	24	3	0	9	3.14
2	4	0	29	100	24	3	0	14	4.01
3	4	0	9	94	39	13	1	2	4.38
4	4	0	16	103	35	2	0	8	4.15
5	3	0	13	85	57	1	0	5	3.30
6	5	7	69	73	7	0	0	18	4.51
7	5	5	51	73	18	4	5	17	4.89
8	4	0	28	89	35	4	0	10	4.10
9	3	0	25	103	25	2	1	12	3.05
OUT	35	12	248	841	264	32	7		35.50
10	4	0	17	116	22	1	0	12	4.05
11	5	0	49	77	24	5	1	6	4.94
12	3	0	10	84	58	3	1	3	3.37
13	4	2	34	93	22	5	0	15	3.96
14	4	0	14	80	56	5	1	1	4.35
15	4	0	5	85	56	9	1	4	4.47
16	4	0	26	99	28	3	0	11	4.05
17	4	0	11	101	37	6	1	6	4.26
18	4	0	20	93	37	6	0	7	4.19
IN	36	2	186	828	340	43	5		37.63
TOTAL	71	14	434	1669	604	75	12		73.13

Players Below Par	33
Players At Par	18
Players Above Par	105

LOW SCORES

Low First Nine	Colin Montgomerie	30
Low Second Nine	Miguel Angel Jimenez	33
	Robert Allenby	33
Low Round	Colin Montgomerie	65

WEATHER

Temperature: low 14°C, high 18°C.
Northerly breeze.

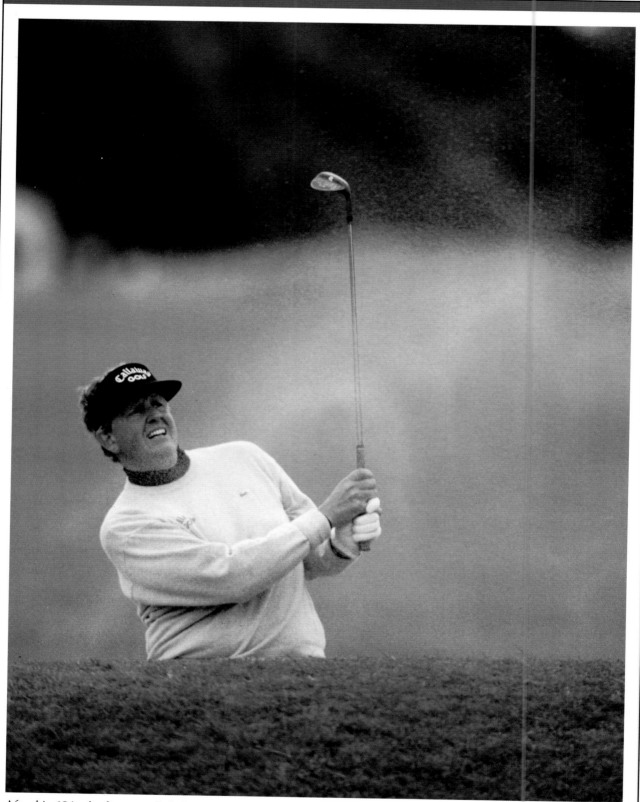

After his 65 in the first round, Colin Montgomerie said, "This, as you know, is a game of confidence."

COMMENTARY

MONTY'S TANTALISING PRIZE

BY MARINO PARASCENZO

Colin Montgomerie, from the moment he stepped on the PGA European Tour in 1987, clearly was supposed to win golf's major championships. It's a burden he brought on himself. He is a man with that kind of talent. He topped the European Tour's Order of Merit for seven straight years. Majors? He should win one, at least. Probably more. Monty himself once said he ought to have maybe five by now, two for sure.

The major championships are the career benchmarks for a professional golfer. But for Montgomerie so far, no Masters, no US Open, no USPGA Championship, and no Open Championship. Monty has played and won over most of the world. And he has come close in the majors. So close, in fact, that during the US Open in 1992 at Pebble Beach, Jack Nicklaus conceded it to him on American television. Prematurely, it turned out.

Except for the secret to golf itself, there is no greater mystery than why Montgomerie has not won.

So it was again in the Open Championship at Royal Lytham and St Annes. Montgomerie led for the first two rounds (65-70), slipped one stroke behind in the third round (73), then sank (72) to a tie for 13th place. Once again, he did a post-mortem. This time, the cause was the five-foot putt he had for a birdie at the 18th hole in the second round—when he was leading. He missed that short putt. He got his par and was ahead by one stroke after 36 holes, but he could have been leading by two. "When I missed that one, the writing was on the wall," Monty said. "It undermined my confidence."

Leading by one stroke, with 36 holes to play, Montgomerie was already whipped?

This Open Championship was so close. Montgomerie shot a six-under-par 65 in the first round, not only his best Open start ever, but his first under 70. He led by one stroke. He shot 70 in the second round, still led by a stroke, and was looking over his shoulder at Tiger Woods. "What is he, three under? Four under?" Montgomerie asked. Three under, someone said. "That's great," he responded. "Thank God he's not four under."

Then the old claret jug slowly receded into the mist, like the others. Categorically speaking, Montgomerie may be paired with Phil Mickelson under that heavy title "Best Never To Have Won A Major." But when it comes to being close then missing, Monty is in a class by himself. His record in the major championships is nearly awesome.

The curse began at that 1992 US Open at Pebble Beach. Not that Montgomerie did anything to deserve it. The gods don't need a reason. When Monty finished the final round, Nicklaus, then a guest commentator on the telecast, couldn't believe that anyone would beat him.

Nicklaus congratulated Montgomerie on becoming the US Open champion. Monty was savvy enough not to believe that completely. A number of players were still on the course who could change all that. Still, it had to be an intoxicating thought. Then along came Tom Kite to win and Jeff Sluman to finish second. Montgomerie was third. Things would get worse.

In the 1994 US Open at Oakmont, he tied with Loren Roberts and Ernie Els after 72 holes. In the 18-hole play-off the next day, Montgomerie shanked a chip shot at the second hole, leaving the golf ball in the dense collar of rough. He staggered in, placing a distant third with 78. Els and Roberts tied at three-over-par 74, and Els won on the second extra hole.

In the 1995 USPGA Championship at Riviera, Montgomerie played well enough to win any major, closing with 65 for a 14-under-par total of 267. Steve Elkington finished with 64 and tied him. On the first play-off hole, Elkington rolled in a 25-foot putt for birdie, then Montgomerie just missed from 20 feet. Just missed—the story of his life.

Montgomerie, whose best finish was joint eighth in 1994, had the crowds on his side as he tried to win his first major.

There was a dog-fight down the stretch of the 1997 US Open at Congressional, with four golfers going at it. Montgomerie had made a great come-back from a second-round 76, and on the finishing holes it was down to him and Els. At the 17th, Monty was disturbed by the noise from the specta-tors on the adjoining 18th. He missed the green with his approach, but he pitched nicely to five feet. Then he waited and waited for Tommy Tolles and Jay Haas to finish at the 18th, worried that there would be loud cheers if one of them holed a long putt.

"I didn't want to rush the most important putt of my life," Montgomerie would explain. Finally, it was dead quiet. He missed the putt. He finished second to Els. Maybe he was right. Maybe it was the most important putt of his life.

It was against this roll of close calls that Montgo-merie came to Royal Lytham, bright and bouncy and in high humour. Only a few weeks earlier, he had salvaged a poor year by winning the Murphy's Irish Open. "Having won just a couple of weeks ago, I am coming in here actually with more confidence than I have had for a while," Monty said. He twitted him-self about Open venues. "I don't see it very often on week-ends," he said, "but the first few days it looks okay."

He had played in 11 Open Championships. He missed the 36-hole cut five times, including at Royal Lytham the last time, in 1996. His best finish was joint eighth at Turnberry in 1994. Otherwise, he was joint 15th, joint 24th, joint 26th, and joint 48th.

Those were not encouraging finishes for someone rated as Europe's best for nearly a decade.

Montgomerie grew up playing Royal Troon. Links courses figured to be his strong suit, but so far he played much better in the other three majors, which are played on parkland courses in the United States. Royal Lytham held the promise of being different. It required precise driving and sharp approaches, and Monty owned both of those. Like any major venue, it also required good putting, and his putting had come around.

In the first round, Montgomerie played Royal Lytham's par-3 first hole with ease, a five iron to 20 feet, and holed the putt for a birdie. At the second, a par-4, it was a two iron off the tee to set up a nine-iron second to six feet, and another birdie. He bo-geyed the fifth, then made eagle 3 on the 494-yard sixth, chipping in from 10 feet. He birdied the eighth from 10 feet and the ninth from five feet, and he was out in 30 and on his way to his best start ever in the Open.

He had a carnival on the greens—11 one-putts and a chip-in. He also got a chance to witness, first-hand, the kind of disaster that rarely happens to him. His problem generally is a steady decline. This was Fred Couples self-destructing with a triple-bogey 7 at the 14th. Monty, after watching that horror story, three-putted from 40 feet for his second bogey of the day. "I lost a bit of concentration," he said. He got the stroke back with a birdie at the 18th, holing a 40-foot putt.

"In the past, I always had to play catch-up after the first round," Montgomerie said. "Now I'm in the lead, the whole psyche of the championship changes ..." Then he added, "This, as you know, is a game of confidence."

In the second round, Montgomerie was still steady from tee to green, but his putter had cooled. He had four consecutive birdie chances from the seventh, on putts ranging from four to 15 feet, and missed them all. "It's draining," he would say. "I feel like I have been here 10 days already."

At the 18th, a tough finishing par-4 of 412 yards, he split the fairway with his tee shot, then fired his approach to five feet. The grandstands erupted in a roar. Then he missed the putt. That's when he said the handwriting was on the wall.

Did Montgomerie talk himself out of this Open, or was he being realistic? He escaped the third round with his sense of humour intact, but without his lead. He shot 73, and tried to look on the bright side. "I was very relaxed," he said. "I just putted particularly poorly on the first nine.

"My goal at the start of the week was to get into contention on Sunday, and that is what I have achieved. ... I'm not in the lead, but that could be beneficial. I might be more relaxed. I know I can shoot 65 here because I've proved it already. If I can do it again, I'll have every chance of winning."

Montgomerie was one stroke behind, tied for fifth place with eight others. His final round was all about looking back. "If you are confident of doing something, you will achieve it," he had said after his opening 65. "If you think you are going to do something, you are halfway to achieving it. And that is what I am and I was today."

Then Montgomerie limped in with 72 in the final round. The 10th hole pretty well summed up his day. He had a 30-foot putt for birdie. He slammed it five feet past the hole, then he missed coming back and made bogey. When he left the 18th green, having fallen to a tie for 13th place, he recalled the five-footer he missed at the 18th in the second round. "The writing was on the wall then," Monty said again. "I never felt comfortable with the putter after that."

Montgomerie was steady from tee to green.

Jesper Parnevik (137) represented a formidable threat with his 69-68 start, having finished second in the Open twice.

CHALLENGERS CLOSE IN

BY ROBERT SOMMERS

Always a consideration in an Open Championship, the weather turned pleasant overnight. Where an overcast covered the skies and a cool wind swept over the links for the first round, the clouds had gone, the sun shone bright, the temperature climbed, the wind died, and the scores tumbled.

At the end of the day, 30 men had scored in the 60s, three played the first nine in 31 strokes, and balls seemed to be flying into the hole from all over. Well, not really, but Frank Lickliter scored a hole-in-one on the fifth and Peter Lonard holed a full shot and eagled the 13th.

And Colin Montgomerie still led the Open, although his grin had shrunk and his brow had furrowed because his game's sharp edge had worn dull. Montgomerie followed his marvellous opening round of 65 with 70 in the second, and while the three-stroke lead he coddled overnight had withered to one, he still had command; no one had snatched it away.

Des Smyth, a 48-year-old Irishman, gave it a good run by shooting 65, the lowest score of the day, but he had started too far back to alarm Montgomerie. It did, though, jump him into a tie for ninth at 139.

Those closest to Montgomerie after 18 holes—Brad Faxon, Chris DiMarco, and Mikko Ilonen, who had shared second place overnight—lost ground. Faxon matched par 71 and with 139 dropped into a tie for ninth, DiMarco shot 74 and fell into a tie for 35th, and Ilonen tied for 48th after shooting 75.

Others moved up to take their places. The Swede Pierre Fulke made the most significant move. Shooting 67, Fulke broke out of the 16-man horde bunched in fifth place and jumped into second, and Jesper Parnevik, along with the relatively unknown Englishman Greg Owen and the even less known American Joe Ogilvie, each shot 68 and shared third place.

Montgomerie led at 135, with Fulke at 136, and Parnevik, Owen, and Ogilvie at 137.

Even though, with the exception of Parnevik, he held a good lead over the more dangerous players, all was not serene with Montgomerie. He was developing a crick in his neck looking over his shoulder for Tiger Woods. That was entirely understandable; after all, Woods is the most dangerous player in the game, capable of shooting any score at all.

While Woods didn't burn the grass off the fairways that day, he played well enough to justify Montgomerie's concern. Woods was amongst those who shot 68, a round that jumped him seriously close, to 139, just four strokes behind.

Montgomerie had been watching out for Woods all the way round Royal Lytham, but his name never made it onto the leaderboard. His day over, Montgomerie asked, "What is he, three under? Four under?"

Told Woods had shot 139, three under par, Montgomerie seemed relieved.

"That's great," he said. "Thank God he's not four under." At this stage of the championship, Montgomerie had others to worry about as well. Parnevik, only two strokes behind, had built a much better Open record than Montgomerie's own, which wasn't hard to do, and had been around at the finish of both the 1994 championship at Turnberry, where Nick Price holed a mile-long eagle putt on the 17th to beat him, and the 1997 Open at Troon, where he had held the 54-hole lead but lost eight strokes to Justin Leonard's blazing 65 finish.

Mark O'Meara, the 1998 champion, stood alongside Woods at 139, along with Darren Clarke and five others. Nick Price, Bernhard Langer, and Ian Woosnam, three old warriors, lurked another stroke behind at 140. Price had lit up the leaderboard early in the day by going out in 31. Thirteen years earlier he had battled Seve Ballesteros to Lytham's final green, where Ballesteros administered the coup de grace with a wonderful chip that on video tape still looks as if it might fall.

Colin Montgomerie (135) was running more on the strength of exceptional putting than precise ball-striking.

Hardly anyone noticed Niclas Fasth sitting quietly at 138 after a pair of 69s or David Duval back there in joint 35th place after shooting a dull 73, the kind of round common to him on the big occasions, for a total of 142. He had given no hint of what lay ahead.

Nor did many notice Davis Love III just five strokes behind at 140 after shooting one of the three 67s. If he were ever to win an Open, Love would have liked best to win at Royal Lytham, because it was there in 1969 that Davis Love Jnr, his father, tied for sixth place with Jack Nicklaus.

Love recalled that this was amongst his father's proudest moments, sharing a leaderboard with Nicklaus; Tony Jacklin, who won; Bob Charles, who had won at Lytham in 1963; Peter Thomson, who had won there in 1958; Roberto de Vicenzo, and Christy O'Connor. Davis Jnr died in an aeroplane crash in 1988.

Love teed off a little after 9.30, grouped with Billy Mayfair, who would be in contention until the end, and Gary Orr, who wouldn't. By the time they struck their first shots, Parnevik had already thrust himself into the thick of it by playing the first nine in 32, which dropped him to five under par, just one behind Montgomerie, who wouldn't begin for hours.

Parnevik began with a birdie on the first, ripping a six iron to 15 feet, ran off five consecutive pars, including a 5 on the sixth, which probably cost him a stroke to the field, but he put a three-iron second on the seventh green and took two putts for the birdie. Two under now, he birdied the eighth, and made his par at the ninth for the 32. Parnevik bunkered his second shot to the 11th but pitched to six feet and birdied again. He was four under for the round, six under for the distance. He had caught Montgomerie.

Through the first 13 holes, Parnevik had hit every fairway except one, but he drove into the rough of the 14th and bunkered his second shot. It was his first bogey of the round. Quickly, though, he won it back with a stunning four iron to five feet on the long and hard 15th. Two more pars and he would shoot 67.

The 17th cost him a stroke. After his five-iron approach flew behind a pair of bunkers, Parnevik tried to play a daring chip between them, but his luck turned against him. His ball caught the edge of the bunker and dribbled into the sand. A good up-and-down saved a bogey, his second in four holes. In with 68, he was five under par, one stroke behind Montgomerie.

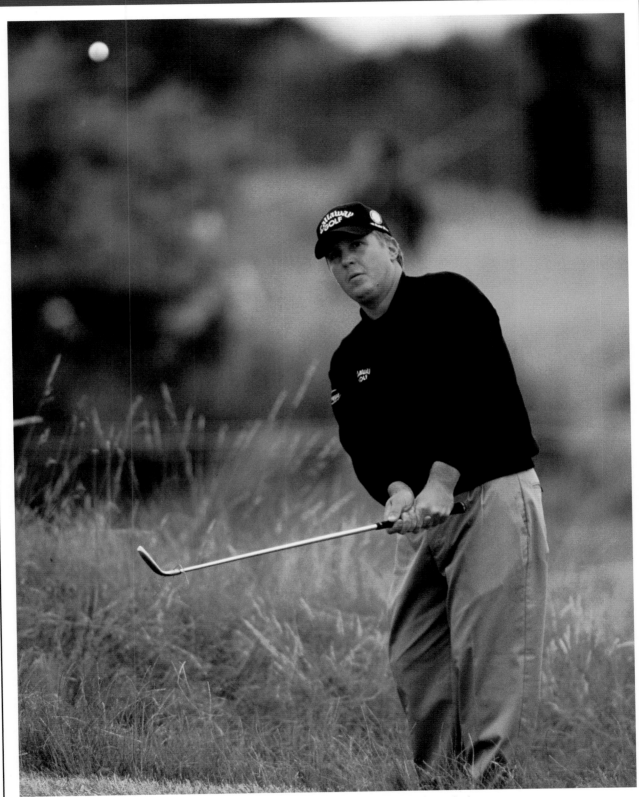

Pierre Fulke (136) had two rounds that contrasted greatly with his struggles through the year.

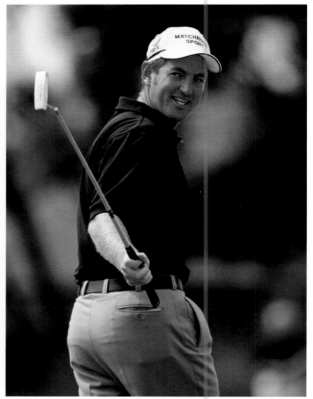

Greg Owen (137) was making himself known.

"The conditions were pretty good," Parnevik said, "and I had to imagine Monty would take advantage of them."

Well, he didn't. While he shot 70, one under par, Montgomerie played tentative golf, which is understandable. Throughout his career he had been under so much pressure in the big events, had come so close to winning without ever pulling it off, it must have been hard to bear.

In an unusually candid moment, Parnevik said he had played a practice round with Montgomerie over the week-end and that Montgomerie hadn't played well. Parnevik said as well that he had asked Alistair McLean, Montgomerie's caddie, if he could explain his awful record in the Open. McLean's explanation?

"He doesn't like the tournament."

Nevertheless, whether he liked it or not, Montgomerie was running ahead, more on the strength of exceptional putting than precise ball-striking.

Taking another huge gallery with him, Montgomerie saved another par from off the green of the first and followed with a routine 4 on the second before running into trouble on the third. His usual slight fade swerved out of control and clattered

Niclas Fasth (138) recorded a second 69.

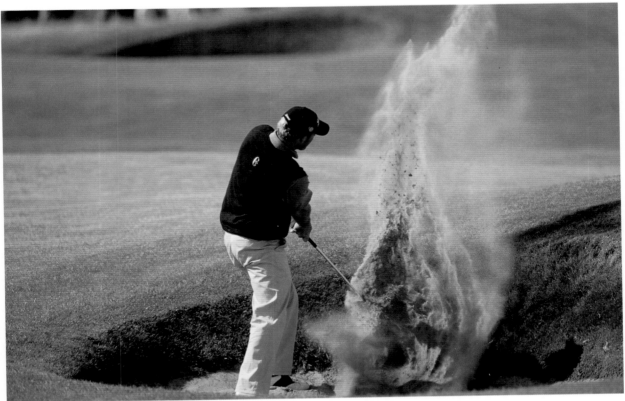

Alex Cejka (138) shot 69 again, but made one of his two bogeys on the 15th after driving into a bunker.

amongst the trees lining the right side of the fairway, just a few yards from the Preston-to-Blackpool Railway line.

Luckily, his ball dropped clear of the trees and he salvaged a bogey 5, then won back the lost stroke with a scrambling birdie on the sixth. His four-iron second missed the green and he chipped to eight feet. On to the seventh, where a strong drive put him in position to reach the green, but he pushed his second shot against a steep bank rising off to the right. Instead of burrowing into the grass, though, his ball trickled out of trouble down the slope, his chip ran eight or 10 feet past, and he missed.

In seven holes Montgomerie had missed five greens he should have hit (even though he was on both par-5 holes with his third shot, they were reachable in two with only moderate effort), and yet he had made his figures. Another opportunity was lost on the eighth, where his lofted pitch settled inside 10 feet but the timid putt pulled up short, then with a routine 3 on the ninth he had gone out in 35, level par.

He came back in 35 as well, with birdies on the 11th and 13th and a bogey on the 15th, where his tee shot ran too far and bounded into a bunker. The

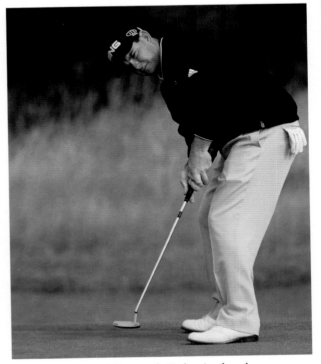

Rory Sabbatini (139) posted 69 despite four bogeys.

41

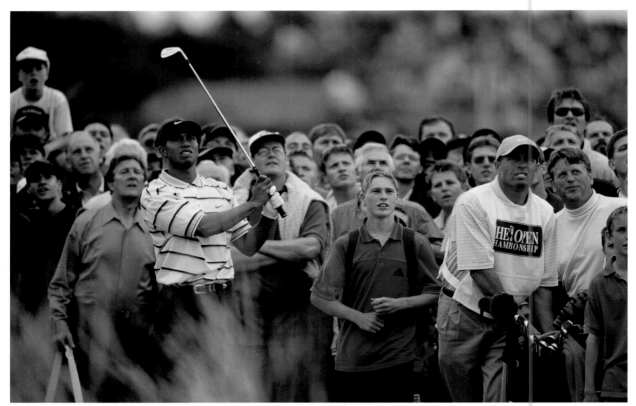
Tiger Woods (139) treated the always-large crowd with 68 in a round with four birdies.

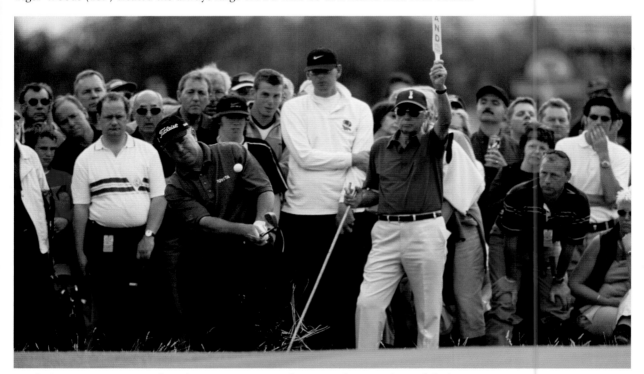
Mark O'Meara (139) scored 69 despite managing only a par 5 here on the 11th hole.

Eduardo Romero (138), with 68, tied his best Open score.

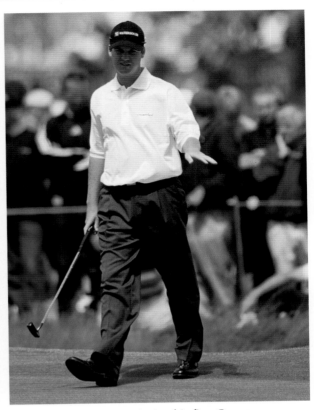

Joe Ogilvie (137) was enjoying his first Open.

birdie on the 11th falls into the category of great good fortune. His three-iron second disappeared into the left greenside bunker, then suddenly popped out and rolled down a gentle slope to the edge of the green. He took two putts and had his 4.

He might have finished with another on the home hole after a lovely pitch to about five feet, but he missed the putt.

The mistake disappointed him, of course, but Montgomerie had made it halfway through the Open still in first place. But like Magellan, he was cruising through unknown waters.

Behind Montgomerie now lurked Pierre Fulke, not only the surprise of the Open but one of its unknown quantities as well. Perhaps he shouldn't have been, since he had won both the Volvo Masters and Scottish PGA a year earlier. Still, 2001 hadn't been a banner year. He had gone to the final match of the Accenture Match Play tournament in Australia early in the year, where he lost to Steve Stricker, but he had missed the cut in three of the PGA European Tour tournaments he had entered, the latest the Scottish Open the week before the Open. He had also missed the cut in the Masters in April and withdrew after one round of the US Open.

At the moment, though, none of that mattered.

A slightly built, 30-year-old Swede, Fulke had played Royal Lytham in successive rounds of two under par and four under par. More impressive, he had bogeyed only two holes—both in the windy first round, none in the second with more difficult hole locations—and in shooting his 67 he had holed nothing longer than a 12-foot putt on the 11th. He had holed from 10 feet on both the sixth and 10th, and from six feet on the seventh. Three of his four birdies fell on the vulnerable par-5s, so he had taken advantage of the openings Lytham offered.

For a change, so did Woods. Unlike the first round, when he parred all the par-5s, he birdied them all in the second. Even so, he was not the same player who had won all those major tournaments. His driving continued to bother him, and the putts no longer searched for the hole so they could dive in.

He did have some luck on his side, though. It seemed that every blade of grass that has ever grown on those ancient grounds is still there, much of it standing knee-high, some of it up to a man's waist. Even if a player is lucky enough to find his ball, shots played from this kind of grass cannot be controlled.

Playing the 14th hole, Woods' drive sailed so far

Darren Clarke (139) lit up in the rain.

Des Smyth (139) shot 65 for the day's low round.

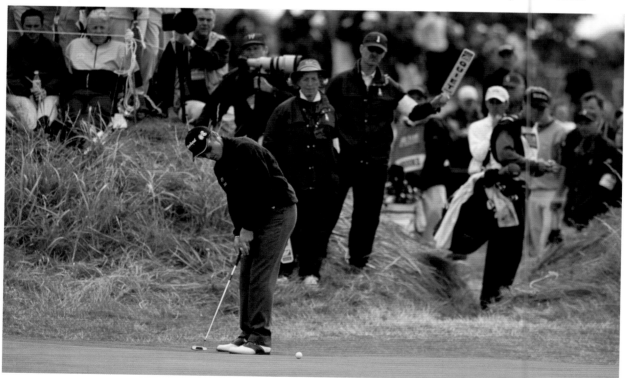

Raphael Jacquelin (139) posted 68 with pars on the last six holes.

right of the fairway it missed Lytham's knee-high rough and plonked down where galleries had mashed the grass flat. When he walked to his ball, he found it in clear view, sitting up nicely about 115 yards from the green. No problem. A pitching wedge to 30 feet, and in the ball went. He made a birdie where anything seemed possible once the ball left the face of his driver.

Woods was four under now and closing in on Montgomerie, playing three groups behind.

One hole later he did well to lose only one stroke. His drive settled in a divot and his five-iron second shot flew into rough so thick he could only hack it into a greenside bunker. A nice recovery to six feet saved the 5, then he finished with three 4s. Once again he had kept himself in position to win without playing his best.

At the same time, two other of the game's more highly regarded players were scoring about as well as their games allowed. Duval had begun the day four strokes back of Montgomerie, playing just behind him. When Duval birdied the fourth at about the same time Montgomerie bogeyed the third, he stood two strokes off the lead. When he birdied the sixth, he had closed the gap to just one.

Right away, though, Montgomerie followed with his own birdie on the sixth and opened his lead to two strokes over Duval, one over Parnevik.

Then, just as quickly as it had taken him so close to the lead, Duval's game turned sour. Lost in the depths of a pot bunker, he double-bogeyed the 10th, bogeyed two more holes, came back in 40, and finished with 73 and 142.

Phil Mickelson had begun the round five strokes back with 70 and, in contrast with his erratic first round, played remarkably steady golf. After missing the first green and dropping a stroke, he birdied both par-5s on the first nine, turned for home in 34, birdied the 11th, the other par-5, and after 13 holes stood two under par. His game collapsed on the 14th. His drive caught the rough, then he hit into a bunker, then three-putted for a double-bogey 6, followed by another bogey on the 17th. Back in 38, he shot 72. At 142 he had matched par and stood alongside Duval.

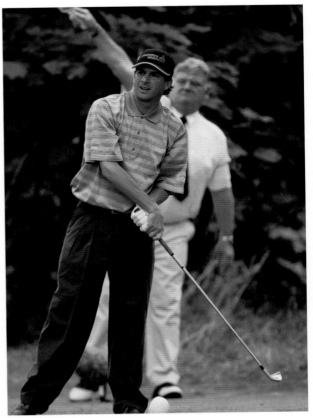

Billy Andrade (139) birdied the 18th for 70.

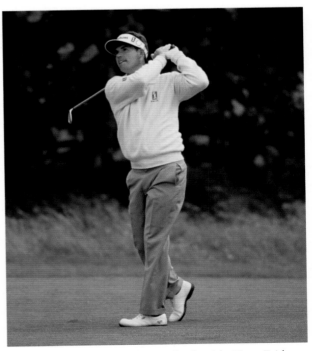

Padraig Harrington (141) came back with 66 on Friday.

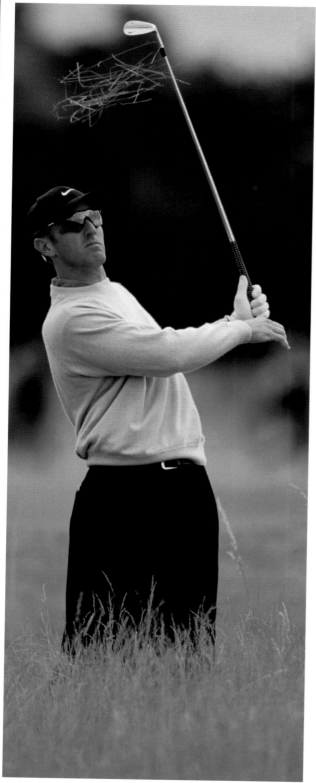

David Duval (142) had 73 and was joint 35th.

While their shaky finishes had disappointed both Duval and Mickelson, at least they would be around for the final 36 holes. A great many others wouldn't.

The 36-hole cut fell at 144, two over par, and pared the field to a level 70 for the last two rounds. It caught some great players of the past and present.

Weakened by a case of the flu, Thomas Bjorn, who had played so well in the important events recently, shot 76-75–151. Mark Brooks, who had lost a play-off to Retief Goosen in the US Open a month earlier, shot 146 and missed by two, and an opening 74 had wrecked Justin Leonard, the 1997 Open champion. With 145, he missed by one.

Then there were those who stirred memories.

Seve Ballesteros had won his first Open Championship at Lytham back in 1979, when he was just 22, catching the imagination of the public as he slashed his way round those old grounds, playing impossible shots, hacking his way from amongst the cars parked alongside the 15th fairway, and beating Jack Nicklaus and Ben Crenshaw by three strokes. Nine years later he and Nick Price battled through a memorable final round at Lytham. Price played the six-hole stretch from the sixth through the 11th in four under par, but Ballesteros played them in six under, shot 65, and won by two strokes.

Ballesteros was 44 in 2001, no longer able to play in his old swashbuckling style. He lumbered through the two rounds in 78 and 71, his 149 five strokes too many.

Ballesteros wasn't alone. The cut caught Nick Faldo, the best player of his time; Tom Lehman, who had won at Lytham in 1996; John Daly, the 1995 Open champion who had come to Lytham with so much hope and left with still another failure; Bob Charles, the Open's only left-handed champion; and Tom Watson, one of only five men with at least five Open Championships.

And who can forget Gary Player's dilemma in the 1974 Open, when his ball lay so close to the Lytham clubhouse he had to play to the green left-handed? He won, nevertheless, the last of his three Opens.

Since Player and Charles had reached 65, this was their last Open appearances as well. It was a shame they had to bow out, but the world moves on.

Amateur champion Michael Hoey (149) missed the cut.

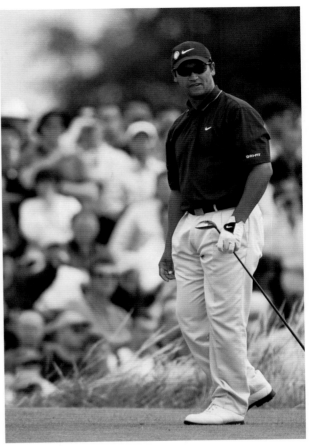

Michael Campbell (143) had not played well lately.

Angel Cabrera (155) was having a fine year until now.

Lee Westwood (143) posted 70 in the second round.

SECOND ROUND RESULTS

HOLE	1	2	3	4	5	6	7	8	9	10	11	12	13	14	15	16	17	18	
PAR	3	4	4	4	3	5	5	4	3	4	5	3	4	4	4	4	4	4	TOTAL
Colin Montgomerie	3	4	5	4	3	4	5	4	3	4	4	3	3	4	5	4	4	4	70-135
Pierre Fulke	3	4	4	4	3	4	4	4	3	3	4	3	4	4	4	4	4	4	67-136
Jesper Parnevik	2	4	4	4	3	5	4	3	3	4	4	3	4	5	3	4	5	4	68-137
Greg Owen	2	5	3	4	3	5	5	4	3	4	4	3	3	4	4	4	3	5	68-137
Joe Ogilvie	3	4	3	4	3	5	4	4	2	4	4	3	3	4	5	4	5	4	68-137
Niclas Fasth	3	3	4	4	3	4	4	4	3	4	5	3	5	4	4	4	3	5	69-138
Alex Cejka	3	4	4	4	3	5	4	4	3	4	5	3	3	3	5	3	4	5	69-138
Eduardo Romero	3	4	5	4	3	5	4	4	2	4	4	3	3	4	4	4	4	4	68-138
Raphael Jacquelin	3	4	4	4	3	4	5	3	2	3	5	4	4	4	4	4	4	4	68-139
Rory Sabbatini	2	5	4	5	3	5	4	4	2	3	4	3	4	5	4	4	4	4	69-139
Des Smyth	4	4	3	5	3	4	3	4	2	3	4	3	4	4	4	4	4	4	65-139
Brad Faxon	3	3	4	4	3	6	4	5	4	4	5	3	4	4	4	3	5	3	71-139
Mark O'Meara	3	4	4	4	3	4	5	4	2	3	5	3	4	4	5	3	5	4	69-139
Tiger Woods	3	4	4	4	3	4	4	4	3	4	4	3	4	3	5	4	4	4	68-139
Darren Clarke	3	4	3	4	3	4	4	4	3	5	4	3	3	4	5	5	4	4	69-139
Billy Andrade	3	4	4	4	3	4	4	4	3	4	5	3	5	4	4	4	5	3	70-139

HOLE SUMMARY

HOLE	PAR	EAGLES	BIRDIES	PARS	BOGEYS	D. BOGEYS	HIGHER	RANK	AVERAGE
1	3	0	10	106	36	1	1	6	3.20
2	4	0	16	108	27	2	1	9	4.12
3	4	0	11	81	46	13	3	1	4.46
4	4	0	14	99	34	7	0	5	4.22
5	3	1	11	117	22	1	2	11	3.11
6	5	1	73	66	11	3	0	18	4.62
7	5	3	74	60	11	4	2	17	4.65
8	4	0	18	104	28	3	1	8	4.14
9	3	0	35	102	15	1	1	14	2.91
OUT	35	5	262	843	230	35	11		35.42
10	4	0	33	100	17	4	0	13	3.95
11	5	1	72	63	12	3	3	16	4.70
12	3	0	11	106	35	2	0	7	3.18
13	4	1	32	108	12	1	0	15	3.87
14	4	0	16	109	24	5	0	9	4.12
15	4	0	13	85	40	11	5	3	4.42
16	4	0	27	109	14	3	1	12	3.97
17	4	0	6	84	56	5	3	1	4.46
18	4	0	14	87	42	9	2	4	4.34
IN	36	2	224	851	252	43	14		37.00
TOTAL	71	7	486	1694	482	78	25		72.42

Players Below Par	47		
Players At Par	20		
Players Above Par	87		

LOW SCORES

Low First Nine	Padraig Harrington	31
	Nick Price	31
	Nicolas Vanhootegem	31
Low Second Nine	Des Smyth	33
	Mark Pilkington	33
Low Round	Des Smyth	65

WEATHER

Temperature: low 14°C, high 21°C.
Light, mainly south-westerly breeze.

The Tented Village provided a variety of facilities including the Open Golf Shop and Show.

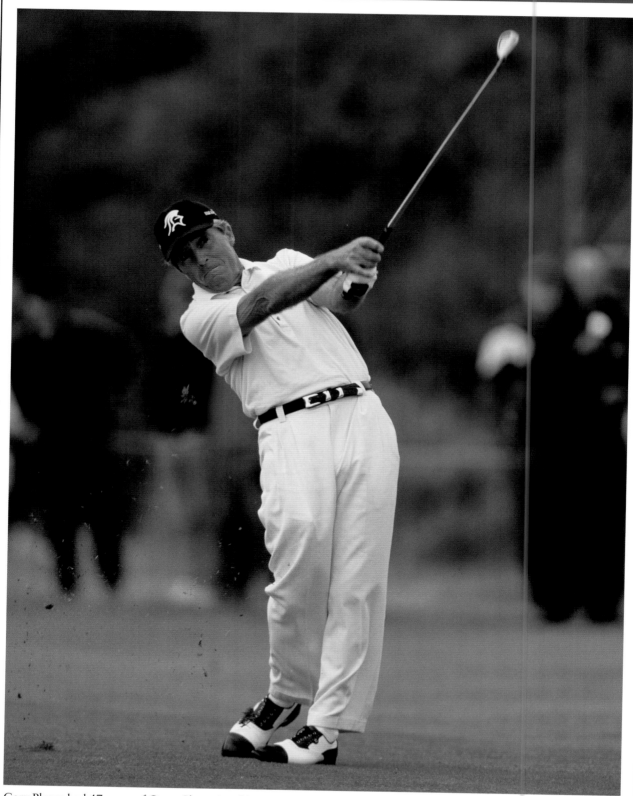

Gary Player had 47 years of Open Championship memories including victories in three decades—1959, 1968, and 1974.

FOR TWO IT'S FAREWELL DAY

BY ANDY FARRELL

It is Farewell Day at the Open Championship. The new champion golfer of the year is always crowned on a Sunday evening. It is on Friday afternoons, however, that the champion golfers of past years—champion golfers for *all* time—are usually acclaimed for the last time. Twice on this day the spectators in the grandstands along the 18th hole rose to their feet to send off, first, a tall New Zealander, Bob Charles, and then a short South African, Gary Player, in the grand manner.

"It was such a wonderful ovation," said Player. "It's something you will never forget in your life."

A golf course is a unique setting for a sporting event and so too is the bond between the great heroes of the sport and its followers. Elsewhere, champions are pensioned off at a much younger age. At golf's major championships, witnessing the modern stars is only one element of the spectacle. Honouring former stars is just as important. It is not just that they were once winners, it is that they have kept coming back, maintaining traditions, providing a link with the past, offering a context for the unfolding dramas.

Paul Lawrie could not add to his championship of 1999 but the Scot will always remember the thrill of being alongside Player at this Open. As the South African approached the final green for the final time, Lawrie shook him warmly by the hand. Even hitting a few chips and putts before the round, Player drew an adoring crowd. Three days earlier, he played a practice round with two more modern major winners from South Africa, Ernie Els and Retief Goosen.

"It was great playing with Gary," said Goosen, the newly crowned US Open champion. "The last hole he was a little emotional. It is probably his last Open and it is a shame. He has done so much for the game and it is great to see him. He played so well today. He was really hitting the ball well. Hopefully, he can pull something out of the bag this week and maybe come back next year."

Paragraph three of the exemption criteria for the Open sometimes undergoes a slight, but important, rewriting. Usually, it says that "past Open champions aged under 65" are exempt from regional and final qualifying. Occasionally, it reads, "Past Open champions aged 65 and under …" This was the case in 1995, when Arnold Palmer was given a final, tumultuous ovation at St Andrews. The revised wording was maintained this year, allowing Charles and Player, both 65, one last tour of duty at Royal Lytham.

It was here that Charles won his only Open in 1963, becoming the only left-hander and the only New Zealander to win a major championship. Player won the third of his Open titles here in 1974, becoming the only man to win in three different decades after his victories at Muirfield in 1959 and Carnoustie in 1968. With five of the eight previous winners at this noble Lancashire links in the field, Lytham was hardly a kind host to its most honoured guests. Tom Lehman, the champion in 1996, missed the cut at five over par, as did Charles, Seve Ballesteros, and Tony Jacklin at seven over, while Player struggled in at 17 over.

"I've had 47 wonderful years at this tournament and I must say I have loved my time over here and supported this tournament to the hilt," Player said. "I love what it stands for. It's the oldest major championship, history is attached to it. I love people and I love golf, but as the Chinese aptly say, 'Everything shall pass.' And it's passed very quickly."

Charles, after competing in his 34th Open, said, "That's my very last swing around Lytham in the Open. I've enjoyed every one of them, but my game wasn't great this week. I'm no longer competitive against these younger players and that is why I won't miss it. It would have been nice to make the cut, but I didn't come close. That's not what it is about anyway. It's all about being competitive. It's time to

Bob Charles remains the only left-hander to win.

denying the remarkable Charles the chance to tie Player's record of three victories. It was the 15th time Charles had played in the event and the 13th he had finished in the top six. It was his fifth runner-up finish, and he was the champion at Turnberry in 1989 and Lytham in 1993, exactly 30 years after his Open victory.

That 1993 victory was sealed with a birdie at the last hole to beat Player and Tommy Horton by one stroke in terrible conditions. He holed a putt from seven feet, but then his putting always was deadly. In the final of the Piccadilly World Match Play at Wentworth in 1969, he beat Gene Littler at the first extra hole after making a 25-footer to square the match at the 36th. Earlier on the second nine, he had holed putts of 45, 25, and 50 feet.

Seemingly, no putt was safe from his silky touch on the greens. At Lytham in 1963, he tied with Phil Rodgers to force a 36-hole playoff, the last in Open history. In the morning round, Charles single-putted 11 times to take a three-stroke lead over the American and eventually won by eight.

Lytham's champions amply illustrate the changing nature of the Open over the years. Though Bobby Jones won the first Open at Lytham in 1926, his successors, Bobby Locke, Peter Thomson, Charles, Jacklin, and Player, are representative of the Commonwealth history of the Open. Then came the European armada in the form of Severiano Ballesteros. Lately, of course, with Lehman and David Duval, the American dominance of the event has returned. Charles and Player both debuted in the Open in the 1950s, before Palmer re-ignited interest from the United States with his wins in 1961 and 1962.

As a South African, Locke was something of a mentor for Player. Neither man hit the ball huge distances but compensated with their mastery around the greens. "Locke never worried about distance," Player said. "He just thought about hitting it down the fairway, hitting it on the green, and making the putts. His short game was immaculate. His victory at St Andrews in 1957 was tremendous."

Of all his Open memories, the victory of Ballesteros at Lytham in 1979 is another to stand out. "That was among the most amazing British Opens I've

retire. I'm going back to the farm in New Zealand to shear some sheep and bale some hay. But seriously, I'm committed to the Senior Tour. Seniors golf is where I am now."

Of course, both Player and Charles have been there since November 1985 and March 1986, respectively, when they turned 50. Player claims as many senior majors, nine, as he won on the regular tour (putting him joint third on the all-time list with Ben Hogan and behind only Jack Nicklaus and Walter Hagen). Player won the Senior British Open three times, at Turnberry in 1988 and 1990 and at Royal Portrush in 1997.

Just a week after the Open at Lytham, Player was reunited with his "Big Three" rivals, Palmer and Nicklaus, at the Senior British Open at Royal County Down. Palmer missed the cut; Player finished down the list; but Nicklaus, on his first appearance at the age of 61, was third, three strokes out of a play-off between Ian Stanley and Charles. Stanley, a 52-year-old Australian beat the Kiwi at the first extra hole, seen," Player said. "It was miraculous. You can't imagine the places he played from and he still went on to win."

Ballesteros was 22 at the time of the first of his own three Open victories. Some 21 years earlier, two 22-year-olds arrived at Lytham, Player and Charles. For Charles, it was his first Open. He was still an amateur and, when not playing golf, worked in a bank.

"I remember it so well," Charles said. "A lot has happened in the meantime." Charles had won the New Zealand Open in 1954, the first of four wins in his national championship, but did not turn professional until 1960.

He finished runner-up twice in the Open, in 1968 and 1969, and won five times on the US PGA Tour, as well as in Europe and South Africa, before embarking on a successful career on the US Senior PGA Tour, where he became the first player to pass $5 million in earnings. Naturally right-handed, he learnt to play the game by picking up some spare clubs of his parents, both of whom also played left-handed. So far he belongs to an exclusive club.

"We are in a minority," he said. "The odds are against us. We're outnumbered, but it's only a matter of time before someone like Phil Mickelson, Steve Flesch, or Mike Weir wins a major."

Player first tried to qualify for the Open at St Andrews in 1955. He made his debut at Hoylake the following year, finishing fourth, and two years later was seventh at Lytham. While Charles was just happy to be there, it was then that Player first appreciated what it would be to win. He watched through the window of the secretary's office as Thomson won and said to himself, "I have to win this championship. I want to win it so badly."

The son of a gold miner would do just that a year later. Player improved his score each day at Muirfield, closing with a 68 that included a 6 at the last. He was distraught after signing his card, but his challengers faded away and he won by two. The legend of the little man in black, one of the first players to constantly work on his fitness and take care of his diet, was born. He won 13 South African Opens, seven Australian Opens, and five World Match Play Championships.

He won the US Masters three times, in 1961, 1974, and 1978, when he came home in 30 strokes for a final round of 64. He won the USPGA Championship in 1962 and 1972 and the US Open in 1965. At the time, he was only the third player to have won all four of the Grand Slam titles in his career, following Gene Sarazen and Ben Hogan. Nicklaus and, at the 2000 Open, Tiger Woods have also achieved the feat. Counting all the titles Player has won, both on the regular and senior tours, the total is in the region of an astonishing 167.

Modern players who tire of travel have little idea of what Player had to go through to gallop round the world. "We had to win the damn tournament to break even," Player said. "With six children it is a different deal, three hotel rooms, a nanny, 33 pieces of baggage, and no prize money, and they all ate like hell."

And then there are all the advances in technology. "How Nicklaus would have played," he marvels, "if you had given him a metal head, all those grooves, lightweight shafts, beautifully conditioned golf courses, his own jet, and $3 million to play for every week?"

A happier memory was his win at Carnoustie in 1968. "There were about five of us within one shot and I was at the Spectacles, the 14th hole, and hit a three wood to six inches," Player said. He went on to win by two from Nicklaus and Charles.

"The windiest weather I ever played in at the Open was when I won here in 1974, without question. The wind was really howling. I remember Johnny Miller going out of bounds on the 12th, the par-3." Player was five ahead at the halfway stage and eventually won by four, despite playing awkwardly from beside the clubhouse wall at the last.

"This is the ultimate test," Player added. "Of all the majors, this is the ultimate test. You are battling the mind and the elements more in this championship than in the other majors. This is the toughest to win, but I've enjoyed playing in this championship immensely. It has been a wonderful experience and I will treasure for the rest of my life the friends I have made."

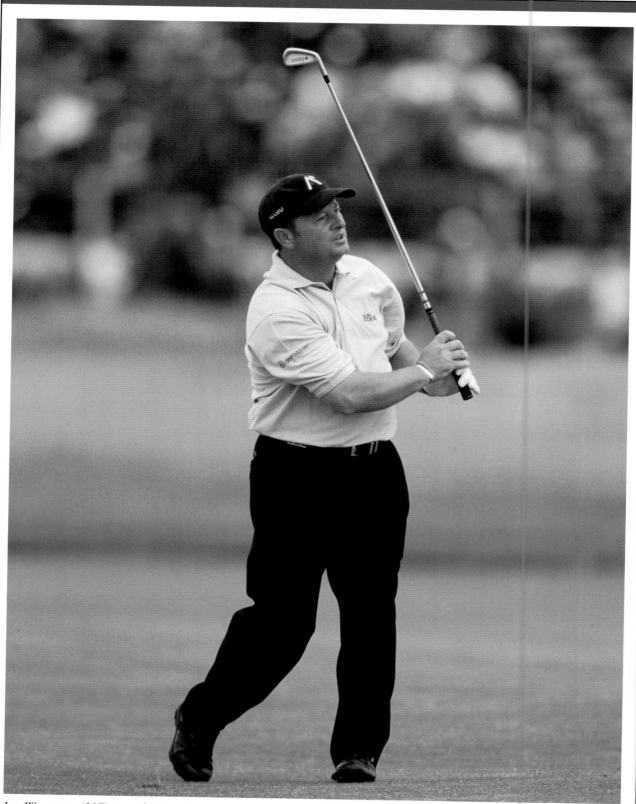

Ian Woosnam (207) posted 67 in the third round as he sought an elusive Open Championship victory.

THIRD ROUND

THIRTEEN WITHIN A STROKE

BY ROBERT SOMMERS

If there had been another Open Saturday like this, it escaped living memory.

This was a day filled with shifting positions. A day when 10 men either held or shared the lead at different times, a day with the field bunched so tightly, one glorious shot jumped a man from 15th place into a tie for second.

It was a day when 25 men broke par, and a day when David Duval asserted himself and when Colin Montgomerie began a slide that ended another futile chase after the championship. Montgomerie began the day in first place and ended it tied for fifth. By contrast, Duval started in joint 35th and ended in a tie for first.

A day when Greg Owen needed no putts at all on the 11th, since he holed a 240-yard three iron for an albatross 2, and when Jesper Parnevik needed four on the eighth.

When it ended, four men shared first place and nine shared fifth—13 men within a stroke of one another. Another six lay a further stroke behind.

Amongst the earlier starters, Duval raced round Royal Lytham in 65 strokes and finished the 54 holes at 207, and in a reprise of another decade, both Ian Woosnam and Bernhard Langer shot 67s and joined Duval and Alex Cejka at six under par. Cejka shot 69.

With the gallery still on his side, Montgomerie struggled with his putter and shot 73, falling into a fifth-place tie at 208 with Jesper Parnevik, Nick Price, Pierre Fulke, Billy Mayfair, Joe Ogilvie, Darren Clarke, Miguel Angel Jimenez, and tall Frenchman Raphael Jacquelin.

Even playing under the constant pressure of the Open, and with his game shifting into reverse as he played the costliest hole of the day, Montgomerie held onto the poise and good humour he had shown through the first two rounds. At one stage he couldn't avoid laughing at a ridiculous situation.

His ball lying close to the sheer wall of a tiny pot bunker on the 13th, about the easiest par-4 Lytham offers, Montgomerie contorted himself into a muscle-stretching stance. With his left foot snuggled into the sand and no room for his right, he bent it at an odd angle over the bank outside.

Believing the seams of his pants were about to split, Montgomerie began giggling and backed away. "That wouldn't have been the most embarrassing thing I've ever done," he said later.

He took two strokes to get out and double-bogeyed.

Meantime, Tiger Woods, who was never out of anyone's mind, roared off to a quick start, played the first six holes in two under par, then hit a wall at the seventh. He took seven strokes, shot 73, and, at 212, tied for 28th place.

The round began on a grey although not unpleasant morning, but towards mid-afternoon the wind freshened, sweeping in from the Irish Sea, the cloud cover lowered and darkened, and the temperature dropped to 16°C.

Paired with Paul Lawrie, the 1999 Open champion, Duval teed off at 11.25, in the best of the weather. Dressed in black pants, a black, long-sleeved shirt, dark blue sweater vest, black cap, his customary dark wrap-around sunglasses, and grim, tight-lipped, unsmiling expression, Duval looked an enigmatic presence.

He had a lot to overcome. He had come so close to winning a major championship in the past, but he never seemed to play quite well enough. Now, after a good opening 69, he had followed with a dismal 73 and, perhaps many assumed, was in for another dull finish.

His first shot confirmed that expectation. It settled in an awkward position close to the lip of a greenside bunker. Was he off on another rocky day? Not at all. Facing a difficult shot, he splashed out within easy

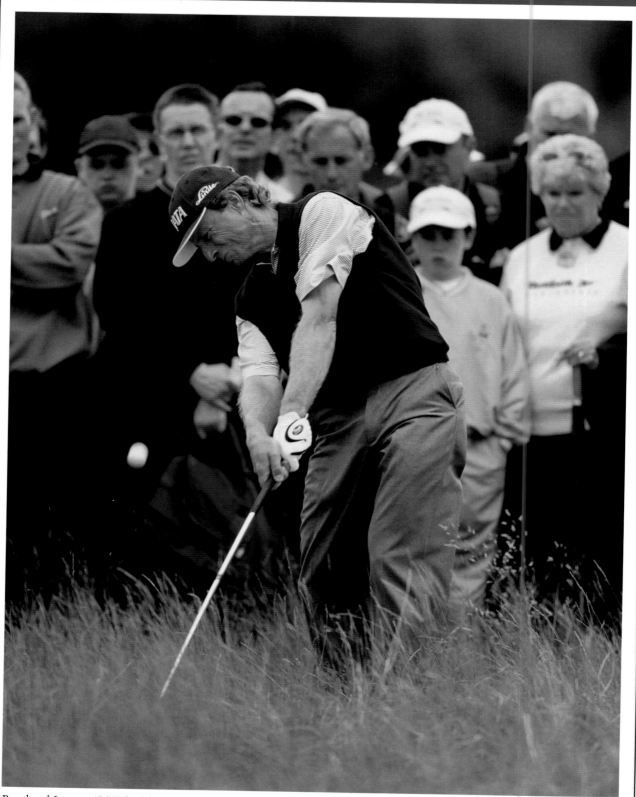

Bernhard Langer (207) had been second or third five times in the Open, and his 67 put him in contention again.

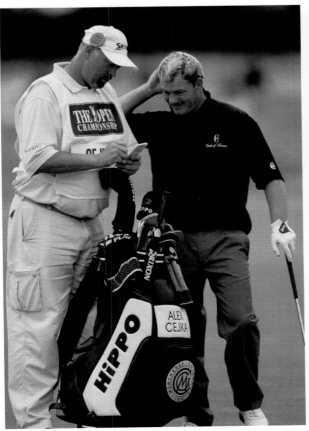

Alex Cejka (207) had 69 with six birdies in seven holes.

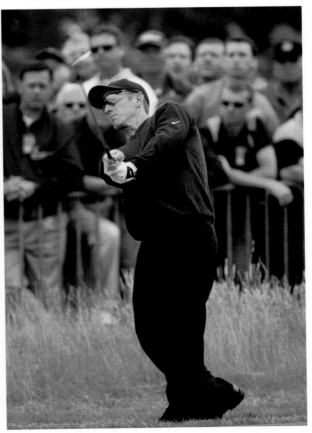

David Duval (207) shot 65, the day's best round.

holing distance, then played a terrific six iron to 10 feet and birdied the second. Although it wasn't obvious at the time, he was off on the most significant round of the championship.

He missed birdieing the sixth, Lytham's easiest par, but he made up for it with a run of six birdies over the next eight holes. Duval began by ripping a two iron onto the seventh and getting down in 2 from 35 feet. Next he lofted a nine iron to 12 feet and birdied the eighth, made his par 3 on the ninth, then holed another 12-footer on the 10th.

He was putting beautifully; balls that had run over the edges in earlier rounds fell in, boosting his growing confidence.

He made another birdie on the 11th, where his five-iron shot settled hole-high off the edge of the green and he chipped to four feet. He was five under par. Safely past the dangerous 12th, he hit a stunning nine iron to the 13th that braked just 18 inches from the hole. Another pitch to eight feet on the tough 14th and Duval had gone seven under par, the same score as Montgomerie.

At the time it could not be said that Duval had

caught up, because Montgomerie had yet to play a shot. Nor had anyone else close to the 36-hole lead. Still, he stood four pars away from 64, and that could work wonders.

There would be no 64. Right away he lost a stroke on the 15th with a drive into grass so deep he took two more strokes to reach the green. He bogeyed to go six under once again.

Perhaps he played his best shot of the round on the 17th, a wonderful par-4 of 467 yards that over the four rounds gave up only 26 birdies, fewer than any other hole. After a good drive, Duval pushed his approach into matted grass about 35 feet from the near edge of the green.

He could easily lose a stroke here. He would have to play a delicate shot across a swale to a hole no more than 15 feet from the edge.

Taking a lofted club, Duval played the shot perfectly. The ball popped against the upslope, jumped onto the green, and for an instant looked as if it might fall. He saved his par and finished the day with 65 and 207.

Duval's golf had been exceptional. He played the

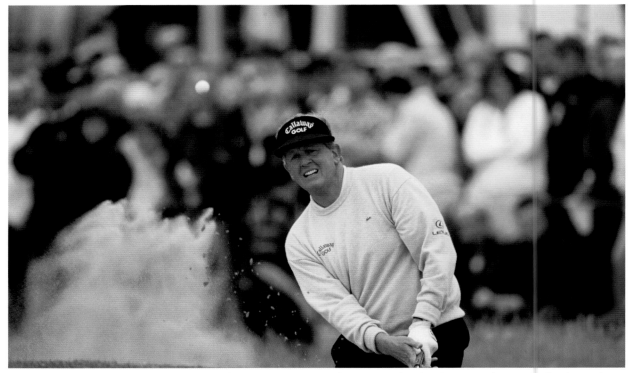
Colin Montgomerie (208) was still where he set out to be—in the running for the championship in the final round.

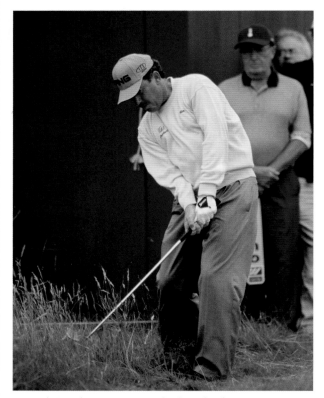
Miguel Angel Jimenez (208) had six birdies.

shots he had to play and holed the putts he had to hole. Still, where the gallery had cheered wildly for Montgomerie—as well as for Woods—they seemed mildly apathetic towards Duval. They applauded his good shots, especially that chip into the 17th, but they showed little enthusiasm for him. That, of course, would change.

When Duval finished, his six under par was second only to Montgomerie's seven under, but with Royal Lytham apparently open to low scoring, it seemed logical that any number of players who had yet to start would certainly pass him.

Midway through the afternoon a few had. After a fumbling start, Alex Cejka had a run of six birdies over the seven holes from the fifth through the 11th and sprinted two strokes ahead of the field at nine under par. At the same time, two others had joined Montgomerie at seven under. The day was turning into a free-for-all.

It had turned quite sour for Tiger Woods, however, not the kind of day he was hoping for. He started well, birdieing the first for the second time, then adding another birdie at the fourth. Five under par now, he was closing in on the leaders even though there wasn't room for his name on the leaderboards.

He gave one stroke away with a poor tee shot short and right of the fifth, then took it back with a second straight birdie on the short par-5 sixth. Now he played the hole that wrecked him.

With a fairway that rippled like an old-time washboard, the seventh stretches 557 yards. But in this age of drivers made of mystical metals from Krypton and balls of mysterious compounds from Dr. Jekyll's laboratory, the green lay within reach of the modern tournament golfer—especially Woods.

Judging from the fury he threw into his swing, he had just that in mind. Luckless, he caught the ball on the wrong lurch. Instead of bounding along the rippling fairway, his ball screamed off to the right, missed safe ground by at least 15 yards, and sank into knee-high grass.

Never one to back off, Woods tore into his second shot, but instead of flying left into the fairway, the ball squirted even farther right into a mass of jungle-like shrubs and trees. Not sure he would ever find his ball, Woods played a provisional to safety, then dived amongst the underbrush like Jason after the Golden Fleece.

Woods found his ball, but it lay in such a hopeless spot he declared it unplayable. With no other option, he marched back to the original position and put another ball in play.

Now he lay three. Two more shots and he was on with a chance to bogey from no more than 10 or 12 feet. When the putt glided past the hole, Woods stared at his ball as if he couldn't believe it had the nerve to miss. He had made 7 on a hole where he would expect to make 4. He was one under now, but more trouble lay ahead.

After a nice pitch to the eighth, he missed a holeable putt for a birdie, overshot the ninth and scrambled for a par, then played a wild second shot to the 11th and parred. He had played the three par-5 holes in one over par where he might expect to play them in three under—a difference of four strokes.

He three-putted the 14th from nowhere, and drove so far into the right rough on the 18th he almost reached the hospitality tents. He had another unplayable lie, but a good shot to the green and a closing bogey.

Once five under par, he shot 73 and, at one under

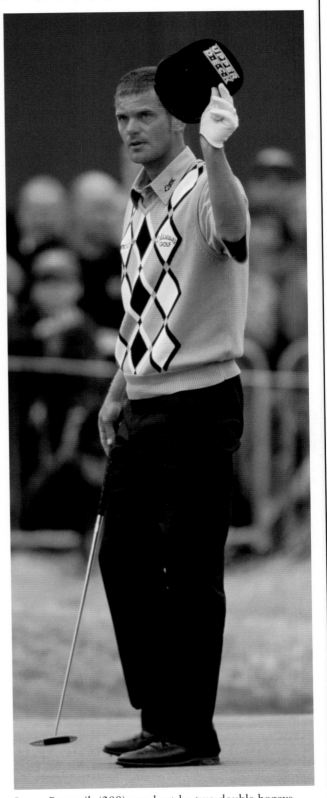

Jesper Parnevik (208) was hurt by two double bogeys.

59

Raphael Jacquelin (208) recorded 69 to stay amongst the leaders, saying he was "enjoying the atmosphere."

Ernie Els (209) was pleased with 67.

par, finished the day five strokes out of first place. With a game like his, he wasn't out of it yet.

Woods aside, the Open now became a struggle primarily amongst nine men, a group that included those old favourites, Woosnam and Langer.

Some years had passed since those two had contended for the great prizes, but on this day they played as they had a decade or more ago. Both had gone to the broom-handle putter and found new life.

Two under par going into the third round, Langer and Woosnam, playing together, started half an hour before Darren Clarke, one of those embroiled in the changing positions. Langer began by birdieing the first while Woosnam escaped a bunker and saved his par. A bogey on the third dropped Langer back to two under, but then he birdied both the par-5s. Woosnam matched him on the sixth, and they turned for home one stroke apart, Langer at four under, Woosnam three under.

Montgomerie had started by then, still in control of the championship. He had led from the beginning, and now the Open was his to win or lose.

Within two holes, though, he had been caught not only by Fulke, playing alongside him, but by Clarke up ahead. Truthfully, Montgomerie was lucky he hadn't fallen two strokes behind, because Clarke had come within an indrawn breath of scoring 3s on both the par-5s. His putt for an eagle on the sixth looked

Billy Mayfair (208) birdied the 15th and 18th holes to finish with 67 and be within one stroke of the lead.

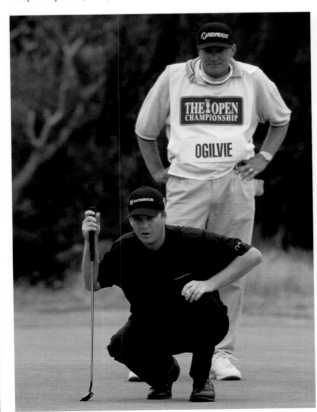

Joe Ogilvie (208) bogeyed the last for 71.

Nick Price (208) shot 68 to move up.

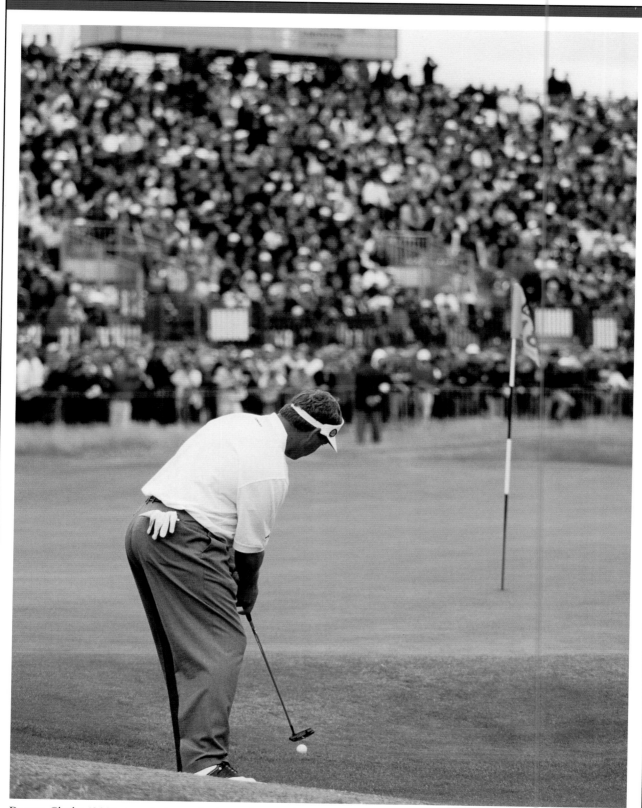

Darren Clarke (208) struggled to make bogey here at the 18th, and his 69 dropped him from joint first.

Sergio Garcia (209) had his best round with 67, despite making bogeys on the 12th and 17th holes.

as if it touched the lip of the hole as it eased past, and his putt for the 3 on the seventh died no more than an inch from tumbling in. Two holes later Montgomerie fell to second place by bogeying the fourth.

Montgomerie had not been sharp. Of the four holes he had played, he had hit only the second green, and yet he had saved pars with a remarkably fine recovery on the first, and he had nearly holed his chip to the third. Fulke, though, had birdied the second and now stood alone in first place.

Up ahead, Langer had started back with birdies on both the 10th and 11th, and Woosnam played a glorious iron into the 11th and holed from no more than six feet for an eagle 3. Langer was six under, Woosnam five under. Then Langer birdied the 14th, Woosnam birdied the 15th, and when Langer's putt for a birdie from just off the 16th green grazed the edge of the cup, he fell over backwards.

At that point, Langer shared the lead with Fulke at seven under par. Clarke had bogeyed the par-3 ninth and stood six under, alongside Montgomerie, Cejka, Woosnam, Frenchman Raphael Jacquelin, Smyth, and Duval, the only one of them who had finished. Now Nick Price had slipped into the mix by going out in 33. It was becoming more difficult by the minute to know who was where in the standing.

Retief Goosen (209) was back near the top.

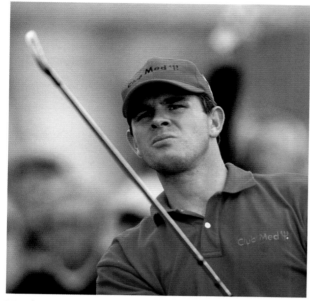

Nicolas Vanhootegem (210) was a surprise.

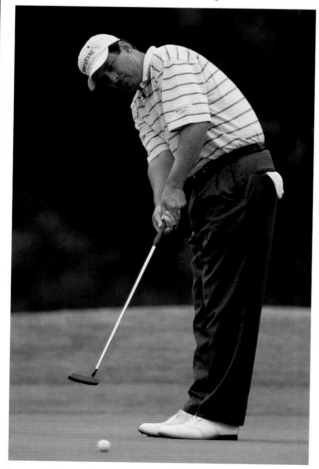

Loren Roberts (210) was steady as always.

Now Cejka made his move. He birdied both the 10th and 11th and suddenly led the field by two strokes at nine under par.

Cejka had had an interesting and adventurous life. Born in Czechoslovakia during communist rule, he and his father escaped when Alex was only 10 years old. On holiday in Yugoslavia, they made their way to a river, swam across, boarded a train, traveled through Italy and Switzerland, and finally found refuge in Munich, in what was then West Germany. Cejka became a German citizen, but he had recently moved to Prague in the Czech Republic.

Amongst Cejka's other accomplishments, he speaks five languages. His golf ball must understand one of them because it had been strikingly obedient so far. He had birdied six of the first 11 holes, with a bogey at the second, but he still had the hardest part of the course ahead of him and what felt like half the population of England closing in. Behind Langer, at seven under, six others stood six under, five more lurked at five under, and four others were four under.

Montgomerie had fallen further behind by then, three-putting the eighth even though a good pitch had left him within holing distance. But he rallied quickly, birdied the 10th after another good pitch, then added another at the 11th. He was back to seven under.

From then on most of those in front fought losing battles to hold strokes they had already won. Cejka bogeyed the tough 15th, then stubbed his approach to the easy 16th and bogeyed again, and dropped another on the difficult 17th—three straight bogeys. With a round of 66 in sight, he shot 69 and finished six under, tied with Duval, whose 54-hole score looked better every minute.

Montgomerie lost two strokes from the bunker on the 13th, and Langer drove into a bunker on the 18th and bogeyed, dropping to six under.

Parnevik, meanwhile, had recovered from four-putting the eighth, run off four straight birdies, and climbed into first place, seven under par through the 16th.

Now, with only two holes between him and the outright lead, Parnevik let it get away on the 17th.

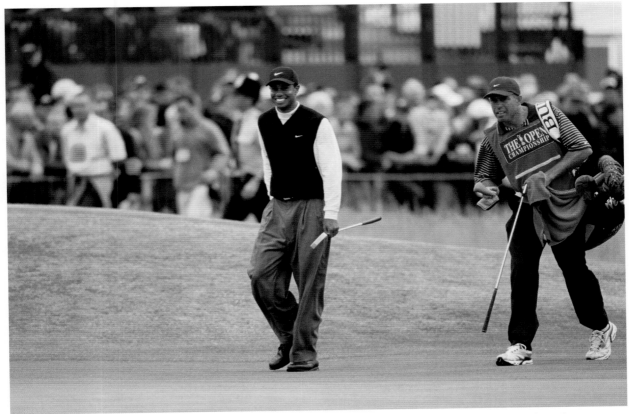

Tiger Woods (212) did not show the frustration of his 73 as he heard the cheers from the 18th grandstands.

He pushed his drive into rough so deep he couldn't chop the ball back into play. His second shot dropped in so poor a lie he dare not go for the green or even try to carry a nest of bunkers no more than 60 yards ahead. Instead, he punched his ball back to the fairway and double-bogeyed, his second of the round. He shot 71 and finished five under.

Clarke had gone to the 18th six under, but he missed the green, bogeyed, and finished five under as well.

Not everyone fell apart, though. Always a fighter, Woosnam rifled a three iron into the 17th and holed from 20 feet for the birdie, one of only five that day. He played the second nine in 33, three under par, and finished six under. Only Duval and Mark O'Meara had played Lytham's brutal second nine as well. O'Meara was back in a tie for 24th place.

At the end of the day, all those predictions that Duval's had been a good effort but that he would still be back in the pack were mistaken. Of the 15 men who had begun the third round within five strokes of Montgomerie, only eight had broken par 71.

Now four men shared first place, each of them with something to prove.

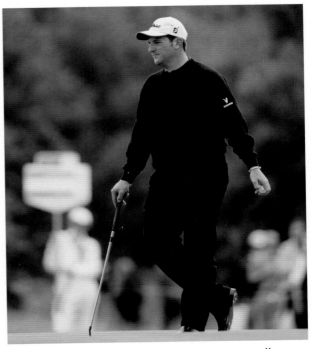

Amateur David Dixon (211) was playing very well.

Caddie Steve Williams and Tiger Woods search for his golf ball as television cameras have an ideal viewpoint.

THIRD ROUND RESULTS

HOLE	1	2	3	4	5	6	7	8	9	10	11	12	13	14	15	16	17	18	TOTAL
PAR	3	4	4	4	3	5	5	4	3	4	5	3	4	4	4	4	4	4	TOTAL
David Duval	3	3	4	4	3	5	4	3	3	3	4	3	3	3	5	4	4	4	65-207
Bernhard Langer	2	4	5	4	3	4	4	5	4	3	4	3	3	4	3	5	3	4	67-207
Ian Woosnam	3	4	4	4	3	4	4	4	3	4	4	4	3	5	5	5	5	4	67-207
Alex Cejka	3	5	4	4	2	4	4	4	2	3	4	4	4	3	5	5	5	4	69-207
Miguel Angel Jimenez	3	3	4	4	3	4	4	4	3	4	6	3	4	3	4	3	5	3	67-208
Billy Mayfair	3	4	4	4	3	4	5	4	2	4	5	3	4	4	3	4	4	3	67-208
Nick Price	3	4	4	4	3	4	4	5	2	4	5	3	3	3	4	4	5	4	68-208
Darren Clarke	3	3	4	4	2	4	4	4	4	4	5	3	4	4	4	4	4	5	69-208
Raphael Jacquelin	4	3	4	4	3	5	4	4	2	3	6	3	4	4	4	4	4	4	69-208
Joe Ogilvie	4	4	5	3	3	4	5	5	3	4	3	3	4	4	4	4	4	5	71-208
Jesper Parnevik	4	3	4	5	3	4	5	6	2	3	4	2	4	4	4	4	6	4	71-208
Pierre Fulke	3	3	4	4	3	5	6	4	4	4	5	3	4	3	6	4	4	3	72-208
Colin Montgomerie	3	4	4	5	3	5	5	5	3	3	4	3	6	4	4	4	4	4	73-208

HOLE SUMMARY

HOLE	PAR	EAGLES	BIRDIES	PARS	BOGEYS	D. BOGEYS	HIGHER	RANK	AVERAGE
1	3	0	8	48	14	0	0	8	3.09
2	4	0	12	45	12	1	0	10	4.03
3	4	0	2	45	17	6	0	1	4.39
4	4	0	11	43	15	1	0	8	4.09
5	3	0	4	52	12	2	0	6	3.17
6	5	2	36	27	3	2	0	18	4.53
7	5	1	35	28	4	2	0	17	4.59
8	4	0	5	42	18	5	0	3	4.33
9	3	0	21	42	7	0	0	15	2.80
OUT	35	3	134	372	102	19	0		35.00
10	4	0	19	44	7	0	0	13	3.83
11	5	4	21	35	10	0	0	16	4.71
12	3	0	4	51	15	0	0	7	3.16
13	4	0	17	49	3	1	0	13	3.83
14	4	1	15	43	9	2	0	12	3.94
15	4	0	4	40	23	2	1	2	4.37
16	4	0	9	52	9	0	0	11	4.00
17	4	0	5	39	24	2	0	3	4.33
18	4	0	9	39	18	4	0	5	4.24
IN	36	5	103	392	118	11	1		36.42
TOTAL	71	8	237	764	220	30	1		71.42

Players Below Par	25
Players At Par	9
Players Above Par	36

WEATHER

Temperature: low 16°C, high 20°C.
Light southerly breeze.

LOW SCORES

Low First Nine	Ernie Els	32
	Miguel Angel Jimenez	32
	David Duval	32
	Darren Clarke	32
	Alex Cejka	32
	Retief Goosen	32
	Sergio Garcia	32
Low Second Nine	Ian Woosnam	33
	Mark O'Meara	33
	David Duval	33
Low Round	David Duval	65

Tiger Woods says whether he plays well or poorly, "It is blown out of proportion. The real truth is somewhere in between."

THE IMPERFECT TIGER

BY RON SIRAK

There is a concept in Zen Buddhist philosophy that says that near perfection is more beautiful than perfection, if for no other reason than because it is attainable. The pursuit of perfection is clearly a road traveled and not a destination reached. And that sage Zen master Ben Hogan once told of a dream he had in which he made 17 consecutive holes-in-one, only to have his tee shot on the final hole circle the inner edge of the cup and then spin out. The message is clear: Even in our dreams, golf is not a game mastered. Victory goes not so much to those who make the most good shots, but rather to the ones who make the fewest poor shots. And mastery of the sport is an elusive passing fancy, a muse that visits some longer than others.

Enter Tiger Woods, the young man who played at such a level for so long it appeared as if he had stumbled upon "the secret" many felt Hogan had discovered and never revealed. In a stunning run of near perfection that began after the 1999 Bay Hill Invitational and culminated shortly following the 2001 Masters in which he won his fourth consecutive major championship, Woods displayed a level of excellence that lured many into believing that this astounding run of greatness was not merely a hot streak, but rather simply the way things would remain for years to come.

Woods had seemingly achieved golfing perfection. It was an assessment that held Woods to an unfair standard, and no one understood that better than Woods.

"The game is very fickle and we try as hard as we can," Woods said when it became clear that the claret jug he captured a year earlier on the Old Course at St Andrews would pass to another in the 130th Open Championship at Royal Lytham and St Annes. "I probably understand a lot more (than spectators) how tough it is, because I'm out there playing and trying to deal with the emotions and the situations you have to deal with down the stretch of a major championship."

In defeat Woods can truly revel in his victories. If the human side of the 25-year-old American was revealed in his lack of mastery of Royal Lytham, his super-human side comes even more sharply into focus. The pause in the Woods dynamo, first in the US Open at Southern Hills in Oklahoma and then at Royal Lytham, gives cause to step back and appreciate nearly two years of nearly perfect golf. Consider the numbers. Beginning with the 1999 Deutsche Bank-SAP Open and ending with the 2001 Masters, Woods won an astounding 25 times in 50 events. More staggering is the fact that in those 50 events world-wide, 45 times he finished in the top 10; meaning, virtually every time he played for two years he had a chance to win.

And nowhere was he more dominating than in the major championships. In that glorious run of 50 tournaments, he played in eight major championships and won five of them. And it was not just the victories he garnered, but the manner in which he accomplished them. In 2000, when Woods won the US Open, the Open Championship and the USPGA Championship, it was by a combined 23 strokes at an aggregate 49 strokes under par.

The closest any player has come to that level of sustained excellence was when Hogan himself won 32 times beginning in 1946 and ending with his near-fatal automobile crash on 2 February 1949. Commencing with the 1946 USPGA Championship and concluding with the 1953 Open Championship at Carnoustie, Hogan won nine of the 16 majors in which he played. In 1953, when Hogan achieved the feat matched only by Woods of winning three majors in a single year, it was by a combined 15 strokes at a cumulative 15 under par.

Truly, these were the standards by which the golfing world had grown used to judging Woods. His

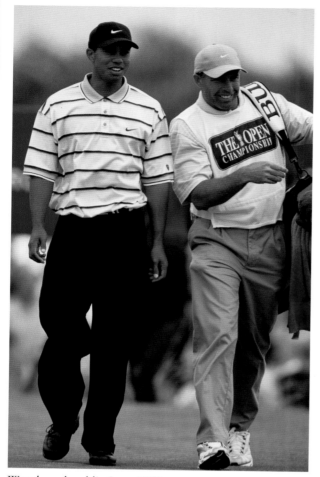

Woods and caddie Steve Williams are a team.

try on No 10, and three-putted the 11th for a par. Employing the swing of a desperate man clearly feeling his chances slipping away, Woods hit the deep rough on the par-3 12th hole on his way to a triple-bogey 6.

"I'm not thrilled that I wasn't able to contend down the stretch, but I had my chances out there today," Woods said after the final round. "If I had birdied seven with a nine iron in my hand and if I had got three or four more coming in, you never know."

If truth be told, the day that ended his chances was Saturday. He started the third round with only eight players in front of him and finished the round trailing 27 other golfers. This was not the kind of Saturday performance we had come to expect from Woods in a major championship. The fact that he managed to scratch out a 73 in a round in which he hit only seven fairways and missed seven greens showed the resiliency his game has developed as he has matured both as a player and as a person. Clearly frustrated by the day's play, he was tight with his words after.

"Today was a frustrating round because I had it going early for a little while and got to five under par (he made birdies on three of the first six holes), but I hit a couple of squirrely shots and had a couple of unplayable lies today and really didn't drive the ball very well," Woods said.

The momentum was lost on No 7 on Saturday when he drove the ball into the right rough and then hit his second shot farther right, ending with an unplayable lie penalty. The result was a double-bogey 7. Following that disaster he made no more birdies over the final 11 holes and struggled to limit the damage to a two-over-par 38 on the back nine.

"I wasn't feeling comfortable with my swing today and unfortunately it showed," he said.

No sooner were those words out of his mouth than Woods turned his back on the clubhouse, summoned his caddie Steve Williams and coach Butch Harmon, and headed for the practice range. Standing in the fading light on the near-empty facility, Woods hit a couple of wedges and a few seven irons, then went right for the driver. His first three swings resulted in

opponents, it seemed, were Hogan and Jack Nicklaus and Bobby Jones and Harry Vardon, the players who dominated earlier generations. It seemed as if history was a blank page set before Woods upon which he could write in his accomplishments at will. And Woods at his peak is exactly that unique performer. If there is solace to be gained in witnessing Woods struggle with his game like a mere mortal, it is in grasping how brilliant he is when he is at his best.

Playing far from his peak at Royal Lytham—he struggled with the driver mightily the first three rounds—it was somewhat amazing that Woods was still in the hunt until two-thirds of the way through the final round. Starting the final 18 holes five strokes off the lead (he had erased greater deficits in fewer holes), Woods made a move with birdies on Nos 4, 5, and 6. It was then that the fickle side of the game paid Woods an untimely visit. He failed to birdie the par-5 seventh hole, despite having a nine iron in his hands for his second shot, missed a nine-foot birdie shots that curved wildly to the right, this time clang-ing off the chain-link fence that defined the range instead of burying in the rough as they had on the course.

In clear frustration, Woods shrugged his shoulders, looked quizzically at Harmon, and placed his arm on his golf bag and bent forward wearily, resting his head in the crook of his elbow. With a sigh he stood back tall, stuck out his hand for another ball from Williams, and hit another shot. And another. And another. It was an hour later before he ceased his practice.

After loading his clubs in his car, Woods and Williams climbed into separate vehicles. The player turned to the caddie and said, "Call me." Clearly there was more to discuss. Somehow, with the help of those closest to him, he would sort this out and reclaim the magic he possessed for two years.

There is a harmonious symmetry to the fact that Woods struggled in his return to Royal Lytham, the place where he played his final Open Championship as an amateur. Indeed, in his previous visit to the storied links where for many years Bobby Jones was the lone American champion, Woods found something that was the springboard for his professional career. Earl Woods points to the second round of the 1996 championship at Royal Lytham as when he knew that his son was ready to turn professional. The then 20-year-old amateur posted a 66 and followed that with a pair of 70s to finished tied for 22nd place.

"That's when I knew he was ready to play with the big boys," Earl Woods said, "because that's when I knew that he knew he could beat them all."

The younger Woods remembers that week with absolutely clarity.

"That round, my swing really came together," he said as he thought back during his most recent visit to Lytham. "If I wanted to put it over here, I was able to put it here. If I wanted to put it here with this shape, I was able to do that. To do that in a major championship atmosphere gave me the confidence to know I could do it down the road and hopefully to do it as a professional career."

Five weeks later, after winning his third consecu-tive US Amateur championship, Woods turned professional. And five weeks after that he had his first professional victory.

Early in the week there were clear indications that Woods had not come to Lytham with what he likes to call his "A" game. On Tuesday he and Harmon worked with a video camera to try to pinpoint the flaws in his technique.

An opening-round 71 in quite windy conditions and in which he made birdies on none on the par-5 holes seemed to position Woods nicely. That particularly seemed to be the case when he followed up with 68 on Friday, making birdies on all three of the par-5 holes to get to three under par, just four strokes off the pace set by Colin Montgomerie.

Woods appeared to be perfectly poised for a Saturday run that would put the added pressure on the other players of knowing that they would have to chase down Tiger on Sunday. That was not to be. There was no miracle in the making this time. Still, it is a mark of the greatness of the man that even when he is off his form, he can achieve a top-25 finish in this most difficult of championships. And it is a mark of the greatness of the man that people have come to expect so much from him, at times unrealistic expectations that he understands so very well.

"When I play well I think it is blown out of proportion a little bit," Woods said. "I think when I play poorly it is blown out of proportion. The real truth is somewhere in between."

The real truth is that Woods is every bit as good as everyone says he is when he is playing well. And one proof of that is how well he performs even when people say he is playing poorly. At Royal Lytham he was in contention for 65 holes, a position almost anyone else would accept on almost any year.

Truly, that is all that need be said about him. Woods did not win the Open Championship in 2001, and in that failure he perhaps achieved a lasting victory in that it brought into clearer focus his remarkable achievements of the previous two years. And it made those who truly appreciate the game of golf nod their heads knowingly, smile, and await the next run of greatness when Woods flirts with golfing perfection.

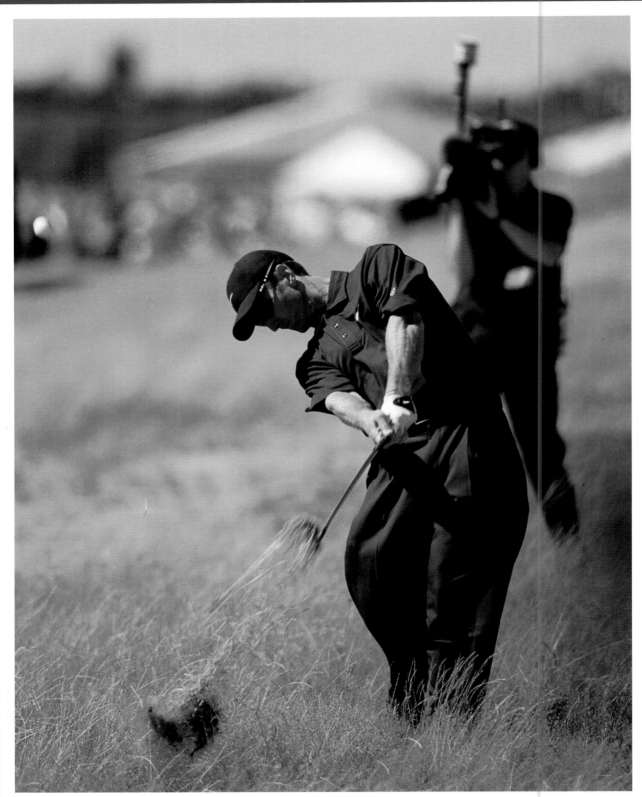

David Duval (274) birdied the par-4 third and par-5 sixth (above) and seventh holes to seize the lead.

DUVAL TAKES COMMAND

BY ROBERT SOMMERS

Halfway through the 1956 US Open Championship, Peter Thomson led Ben Hogan by one stroke. At that point someone asked Hogan, "Would you rather be one stroke behind or one stroke ahead?"

With those cold, grey eyes glaring at the unfortunate soul foolish enough to ask such a question, Hogan answered with a question of his own. "Would you rather be rich or would you rather be poor?"

Obviously, everyone would rather be rich, but as it turned out, Cary Middlecoff became the richest man that week. He won, Hogan tied for second, and Thomson tied for fourth. But Hogan had made his point.

As the fourth round of the 2001 Open Championship reached its climactic stage, David Duval demonstrated quite clearly that he, for one, would much rather be rich than poor. Once he birdied the par-4 third and the par-5 sixth and seventh holes, moving into first place at nine strokes under par, he had opened a gap no one could close. He stood two strokes ahead of Niclas Fasth, playing 10 holes ahead, and except for a brief moment late into the second nine, no one could come closer than Fasth.

When the day began, 19 men stood within two strokes of first place, yet not one of them could keep up with Duval's blistering golf. He simply went out and won the championship.

He won with an unrelenting assault on a course that gave very little quarter, and quite rightly boasts a finish amongst the strongest in championship golf. Duval's closing two rounds of 65-67–132 missed the record for the lowest final 36 holes in any Open by two strokes, but it bettered the best closing 36 holes at Royal Lytham and St Annes by three strokes. Both Seve Ballesteros and Payne Stewart closed with 135 in 1988.

Duval's last nine tested his nerves as well as his playing skills. He held his composure and played one stunning shot after another. When his lead had been cut to one stroke following a 4 on the par-3 12th, his only bogey of the round, he struck back with a nerveless pitch to 12 feet on the 13th, setting up his fifth birdie of the day.

From then on Duval played the shots he had to play while those around him surrendered to the harshness of Lytham's crushing finish. Duval's 67 gave him a total of 274, 10 under par.

In the end, only Fasth, a 29-year-old Swede who hardly anyone realised had entered the championship, finished within three strokes of him. Fasth closed with 67 as well, and shot 277. Six men shared third place at 278, amongst them Ian Woosnam, the short, stocky Welshman who had won the 1991 Masters. Woosnam shot a closing 69, a score tarnished by a two-stroke penalty because of a rules violation on the first hole. He had 15 clubs in his bag.

Miguel Angel Jimenez tied Woosnam for third, along with Darren Clarke, Billy Mayfair, Bernhard Langer, and Ernie Els.

Next on the list in joint ninth place with 279s were two of the crowd favourites, Sergio Garcia and Jesper Parnevik, along with the surprising Mikko Ilonen and Kevin Sutherland.

After leading through the first two rounds, Colin Montgomerie, who had struggled so long to win this championship, closed with 73-72–145 and tied for 13th at 280 with Retief Goosen, the US Open champion, Alex Cejka, who had gone into the final round tied for first place, and five others.

Tiger Woods played the final 36 holes in 144 and dropped into a tie for 25th, his worst finish in one of the four big events since the 1997 USPGA Championship.

In a surprising collapse, Pierre Fulke, one stroke out of first place going into the last round, opened with four consecutive bogeys, scored an 8 on a par-3 hole, went out in 39, came back in 44, shot 83, including a birdie before the big gallery on the home

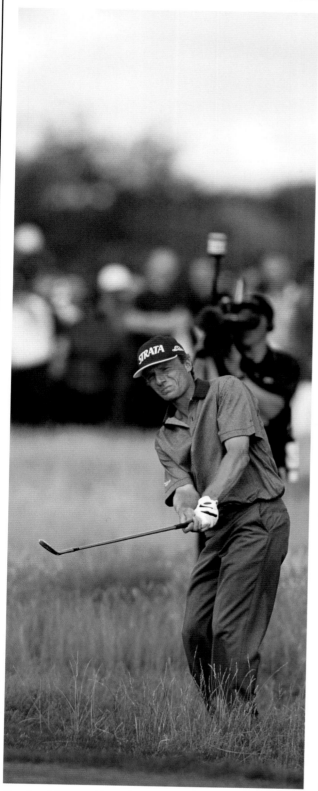

Bernhard Langer (278) finished in level-par 71.

hole, and dropped from a tie for fifth into a tie for 62nd.

Poor Sandy Lyle, the 1985 champion was one over par after two rounds, but he closed with 77 and 81, and with 301 finished dead last amongst the 70 players who completed 72 holes.

Decisive as it was, the victory certainly vindicated Duval, who had been criticised for his failures in the major championships. While he had never doubted himself, he had come so close so often, others questioned his power to win on the big occasions.

Past losses had hurt, of course, but Duval said he had taken a different view of golf coming into the 130th Open. "As much as anything," he said, "I realised it's still a silly old game."

Backing up his new philosophy, Duval had taken a relaxed approach to the Open.

A year earlier, he had joined Woods and O'Meara on their annual pilgrimage to Ireland to go fishing and to play those old and storied courses. Perhaps attempting to take some of the pressure off himself, Duval skipped the Irish trip and scooted off to Sun Valley, Idaho, for some fishing, some running, and some mountain biking. Until he arrived at Lytham, he hadn't hit a golf ball in two weeks.

No one will ever know if it helped, but everyone does know that over those last two rounds, Duval played the game about as well as it can be played. He birdied 12 holes, one of every three, and bogeyed only two—the 15th on Saturday and the 12th on Sunday, neither of them easy pars. The 15th claimed 143 bogeys over the four rounds, more than any other hole, and the 12th took 127, more than all but the 15th and 17th.

Through dedication and application, he had built up impressive strength, but he built his game around more than power. He had the touch to play those delicate little pitches and chips that save so many strokes, and when he putted well he might have holed anything. Throughout the final round he holed any number of the nerve-tingling three- and four-foot putts that can wreck a round.

Still, his power saved a few strokes over the last trying holes, when his driver put him in Lytham's deep and punishing rough. After missing the 14th

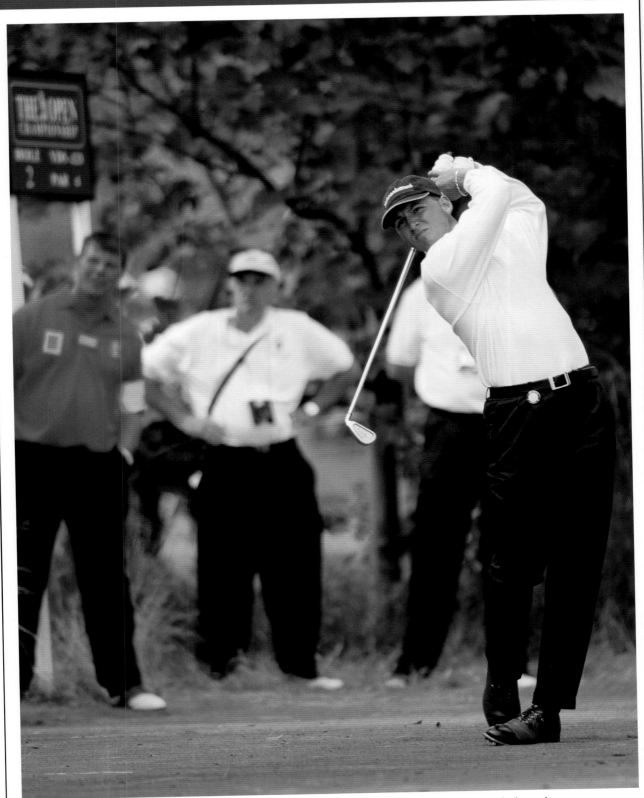

Niclas Fasth (277), in his first Open, was the surprise challenger, and shot 67 to take second place alone.

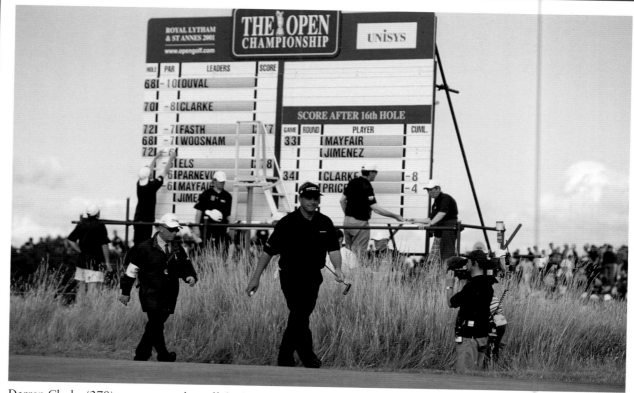

The scoreboard in the image reads:

ROYAL LYTHAM & ST ANNES 2001
www.opengolf.com

THE OPEN CHAMPIONSHIP

UNISYS

HOLE	PAR	LEADERS	SCORE
68	1 -10	DUVAL	
70	1 -8	CLARKE	
72	1 -7	FASTH	7
68	1 -7	WOOSNAM	
72	1 -6		
	-6	ELS	8
	-6	PARNEVIK	
	-6	MAYFAIR	
		JIMENEZ	

SCORE AFTER 16th HOLE

GAME	ROUND	PLAYER	CUML.
33		MAYFAIR	
		JIMENEZ	
34		CLARKE	-8
		PRICE	-4

Darren Clarke (278) was two strokes off the lead before he drove into a bunker at the 17th and took a double-bogey 6.

fairway, he rapped a nine iron from the grass and saved par, then played a shot that astonished David Pepper, the referee and a member of the Championship Committee.

Duval pulled his drive into more rough on the 15th, and from 210 yards out slashed a six iron out of deep grass onto the green.

Pepper couldn't believe it. "If you'd been playing someone who hit a ball that made that sound," he said, "you'd know you were in trouble."

Duval called it, "One of the best shots I've ever hit."

It pulled up 15 feet from the hole for another par. Two more and he had the championship.

As the first man to post 207 Saturday, Duval was the last man off the tee for the fourth round. By then Fasth had passed him. Three strokes behind, at 210, and back in a tie for 20th place, Fasth had gone out in 31 and moved on to the homeward nine at seven under par.

Born in Gothenburg, on Sweden's west coast, across the Kattegat from Denmark, Fasth had played both the European and US PGA Tours during 1998, lost his playing privileges in both, returned to concentrate solely on Europe, and won a tournament in 2000. Now, playing in only his first Open, he showed remarkable poise, especially over the last difficult holes, when he must have known he had the championship within reach.

Fasth started with a rush, birdieing both the first and third holes. When he ran in still another birdie on the sixth, he had caught up, and when a curling 10-foot putt dropped on the seventh, Fasth had dropped to seven under par and taken over first place.

Four holes later, with a birdie on the 11th, he moved to eight under par. Now the field would have to catch him, and if he could hold on, he might take the Open.

All the dangerous players were playing behind him, because, up ahead, Tiger Woods was having another difficult day.

Five strokes back, Woods had gone out in 33, picking up two strokes on par, but any pretense he still had a chance ended on the 12th, the 198-yard par-3. There he played one of the worst holes of his career. His tee shot squirted into more deep, matted grass, his attempted recovery took off scared, scooted across the green, and raced 30 yards down the fairway, and his pitch back dived into a bunker. He took three more from there and scored a big 6.

Nevertheless, hopelessly out of it though he was,

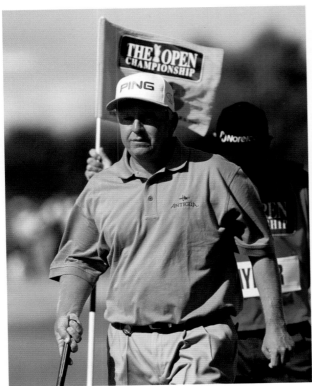

Billy Mayfair (278) made pars on the last seven holes.

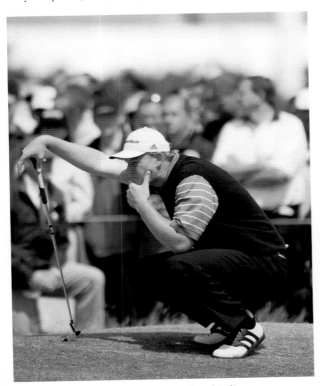

Ernie Els (278) was lifted by two late birdies.

Tiger Woods (283) took 6 on the par-3 12th hole.

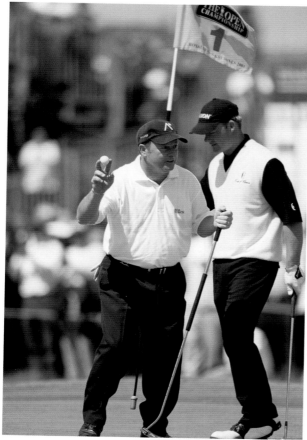

Ian Woosnam (278) thought he had 2 on the first.

Woods never quit. He fought back, birdied both the 16th and 17th, came back in 38, shot level-par 71, and tied for 25th place at 283, one under par. When he holed out on the 18th, the gallery cheered him as if he had won. He had given the best he had to give, but this one time it wasn't enough. The Open would be left to others.

Fasth was amongst them. When he made his par 4 on the 13th, he led Duval by one stroke, and Sergio Garcia, Vijay Singh, Darren Clarke, Bernhard Langer, and Montgomerie by two.

Woosnam sat fuming three strokes back. He had begun with a wonderful shot on the first, so close that for a heart-stopping moment it looked as if it might fall for a hole-in-one. Instead it rolled within five or six inches of the hole. Seven under now, Woosnam marched to the second tee ready to take on the world. There he had a rude shock.

Rushing to the first tee from the practice ground, where he had been testing two drivers, Woosnam had neglected to count his clubs. He carried only one wood, his driver, and so when he stepped onto the

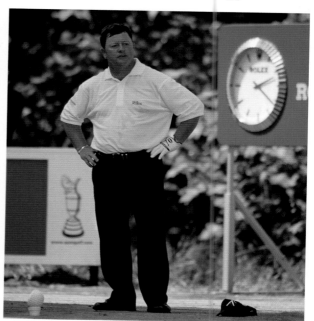

Then Woosnam exploded when his caddie, Miles Byrne, told him they had an extra club in the bag.

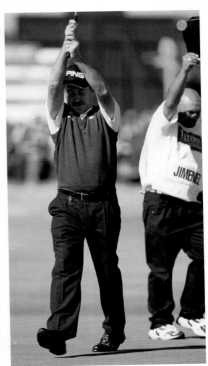

Miguel Angel Jimenez (278) reached eight under with a birdie here at the 13th, then bogeyed the next two holes.

Colin Montgomerie (280) putted poorly on the week-end.   Jesper Parnevik (279) finished with two 71s.

Sergio Garcia (279) managed a par 4 here at the 13th, but could not mount a challenge for the title.

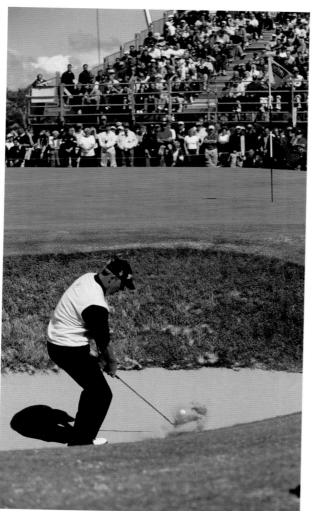

Alex Cejka (280) fell from joint first to 13th.

second tee, his caddie noticed two head covers. The second driver was still in the bag.

"You're going to go ballistic," said the caddie, Miles Byrne.

Surprised and wary, Woosnam asked why.

"We have 15 clubs," the caddie answered, one more than the rules of golf permit. Woosnam was assessed two penalty strokes; instead of beginning with a birdie 2, he had to write down a bogey 4.

Woosnam glared at the caddie, snatched the extra club from the bag, and flung it into the bushes shaft first. It was a bitter setback that never left his mind.

"I felt like I'd been kicked in the teeth," he snapped.

No one will ever know how the penalty affected his game. A long time ago, when the great Bobby Jones was asked if the two-stroke penalty he called against himself in the 1925 US Open had cost him the championship, he said he couldn't truly say it had. He explained that if he hadn't been penalised, he might not have played the rest of the holes as well as he had. In the end, he tied Willie Macfarlane and lost in a play-off.

We do know, though, that after stumbling through the first four holes in three over par and dropping three strokes behind Duval and Fasth, Woosnam began playing wonderful shots. He eagled the sixth and climbed back to five under par, birdied the 11th, bunkered his tee shot on the 12th but nearly holed his pitch, then rolled in a long putt on the 13th. He was seven under now, back in the hunt.

Duval, meantime, had played unyielding golf. After steady pars on the first two holes, he pitched within 18 feet and birdied the third. He stood seven under, one behind Fasth, who had played through the 13th by then.

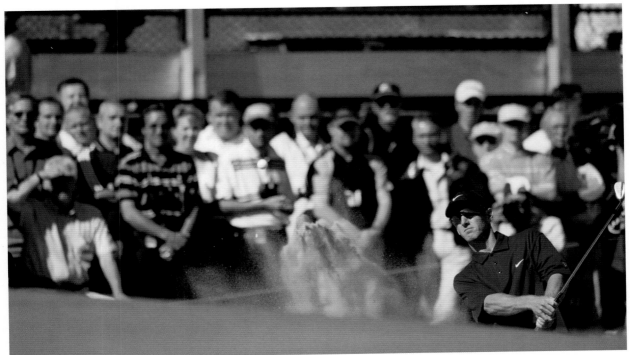

Duval made a birdie 4 on the 11th hole, hitting from this bunker for his third shot to within four feet of the hole.

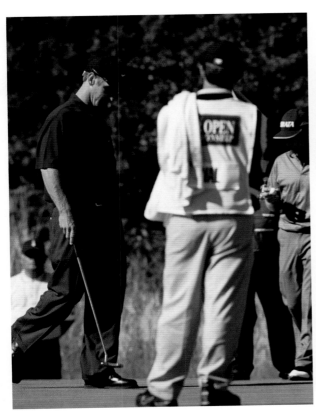

Duval hit into a bunker and took a bogey at the 12th.

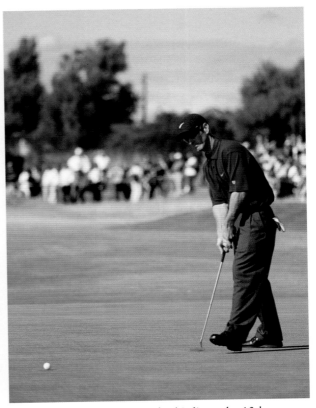

Then he holed from 12 feet for birdie at the 13th.

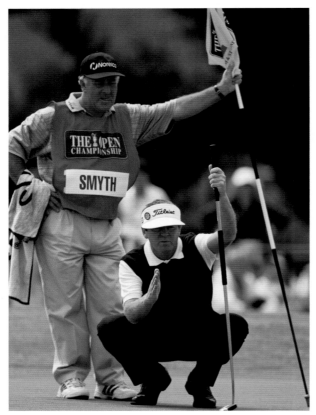

Des Smyth (280) finished with 71.

Now Duval showed his command of trouble shots. His drive in the rough and his approach in a bunker alongside the fourth green, Duval pitched close and holed for the par, and after manoeuvering away from a sprinkler head by the fifth green, he almost holed his chip for an easy par.

Now Duval came to the two par-5s, holes that can either make or break a round. He pulled his drive into the high grass once again on the sixth, tore the ball from the grass with his sand wedge, flew it onto the green, and after a loose first putt, holed one of those nasty four-footers for the birdie. He was eight under par and on to the seventh.

He hit a big drive that must have run an extra 50 yards down the rippling fairway, followed by an eight-iron shot that skipped past a bunker embedded at the base of a mound and ran onto the green. After two more putts, Duval had gone nine under par now.

Fasth had bogeyed the 14th and fallen back to seven under; Mayfair had gone out in 33 and caught

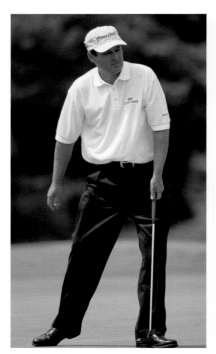

Loren Roberts (280) had four 70s.

Kevin Sutherland (279) had 67.

Bob Estes (283) posted 66.

Mikko Ilonen (279) shot 66 with six birdies.

Davis Love III (281) finished strongly with 67.

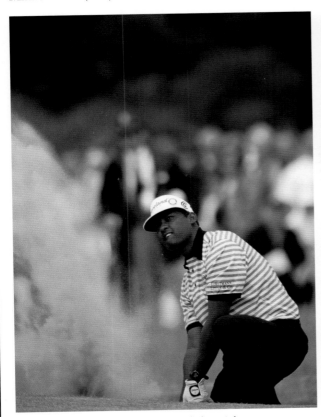

Vijay Singh (280) double-bogeyed the 18th.

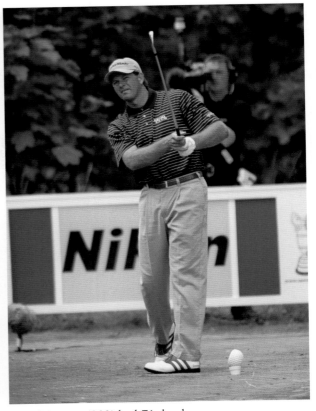

Retief Goosen (280) had 71, level par.

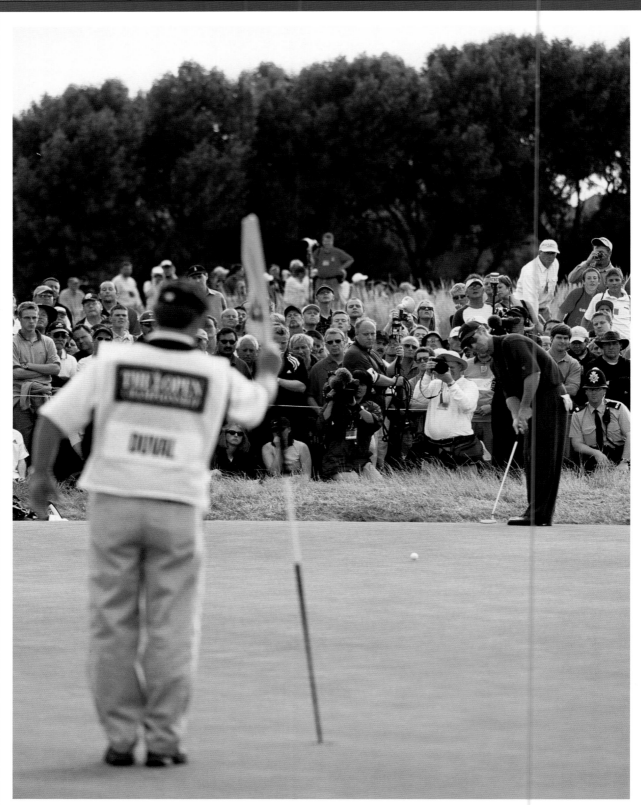

Holding two- and three-stroke leads, all Duval needed was pars on the last five holes.

Fasth; and Singh, Clarke, Langer, and Jimenez all stood six under.

Duval parred the eighth, then floated a pitching wedge inside 10 feet on the ninth, setting up a great chance for another birdie. Instead, he played a timid putt that died short of the hole. He made still another par, though, and had gone out in 32, leading the Open with only the last nine holes to play.

He had made a few mistakes on the outward nine, but, as do all the great players, he didn't let them ruin his round. Now he was about to take command.

He drove into the crosswalk on the 10th, but his pitch hit a few yards short of the flagstick and spun off the green. No problem, he put a little chip inside a foot for another par.

Now he had a mis-played shot followed by another stunning recovery. With his ball lying in the fairway, Duval pushed his two-iron into a bunker by the 11th green, leaving him a shot that had to clear not only the bunker he was in, but another dead ahead. He couldn't have played it better. The ball jumped from the sand, flew over the second bunker, hit the green, and died no more than four feet from the hole. He rammed it home and was now 10 under par.

By now, though, Jimenez had closed within two strokes with his own birdie on the 11th, and he was about to move closer.

Duval caught another bunker by the 12th, but with his ball resting on a slight downhill lie, he pitched maybe 10 feet past and missed the putt to go back to nine under.

Just then Jimenez birdied the 13th, and at eight under par had crept within one stroke.

Just as quickly, Duval birdied the 13th at about the same time that Jimenez drove into a fairway bunker and bogeyed the 14th. Jimenez was finished.

Clarke birdied the 16th to pull within two strokes at eight under par, then played a low, running hook that dived into a fairway bunker on the 17th, hit his next under a grandstand, and after taking a drop, overshot the green into another bunker. With a double-bogey 6, he fell four strokes back. Woosnam had lost another stroke and fallen to six under as well.

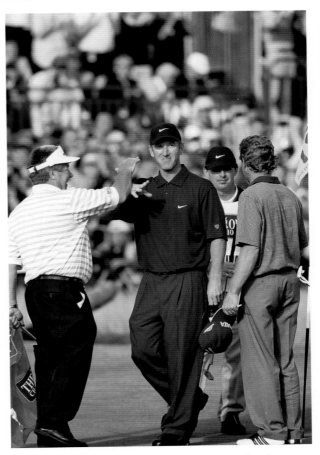

Caddie Peter Coleman (left) and his boss, Bernhard Langer, were the first to congratulate Duval upon winning the Open Championship.

Now Duval had to see if he could hold his game together over the last five holes. He made pars from the rough on both the 14th and 15th, then two fine shots into the 17th and a shaky putt that danced round the cup before dropping for another par. Now for the final hole, played down that avenue between the giant grandstands crammed with spectators.

Few have ever played a closing hole better. He hit a monstrous drive and a glorious pitch within 12 feet. He nearly holed it, but the ball stopped inches away. Duval had won his championship.

When the putt fell, David whipped off his cap and sunglasses, waved to the crowd, and for the first time in public that week, he smiled.

This was a fulfiling moment, because now Duval knew not only that he could beat the best players in the game, but that he could play his best when it mattered most, and that for this one week he had indeed been the best of them all.

FOURTH ROUND RESULTS

HOLE	1	2	3	4	5	6	7	8	9	10	11	12	13	14	15	16	17	18	
PAR	3	4	4	4	3	5	5	4	3	4	5	3	4	4	4	4	4	4	TOTAL
David Duval	3	4	3	4	3	4	4	4	3	4	4	3	4	4	4	4	4	4	67-274
Niclas Fasth	2	4	3	4	3	4	4	4	3	4	4	3	4	5	4	4	4	4	67-277
Ernie Els	3	4	4	5	3	5	5	4	2	4	5	3	4	3	4	4	4	3	69-278
Darren Clarke	3	4	5	4	3	3	5	4	3	4	4	3	4	4	4	3	6	4	70-278
Billy Mayfair	3	4	4	4	3	4	4	4	3	4	6	3	4	4	4	4	4	4	70-278
Miguel Angel Jimenez	2	5	4	4	3	4	5	4	3	4	4	3	3	5	5	4	4	4	70-278
Ian Woosnam	4	4	5	5	3	3	5	4	3	4	4	3	3	4	5	3	5	4	71-278
Bernhard Langer	3	4	4	4	3	5	5	4	3	4	6	3	4	3	5	3	4	4	71-278
Mikko Ilonen	3	4	4	4	2	4	5	5	2	3	5	2	3	4	4	4	4	4	66-279
Kevin Sutherland	2	4	4	5	4	5	4	4	2	4	4	3	4	4	3	4	4	3	67-279
Sergio Garcia	3	4	5	4	3	3	5	4	2	4	5	4	4	4	4	4	4	4	70-279
Jesper Parnevik	3	4	5	4	4	5	4	4	3	4	5	3	3	4	4	3	4	5	71-279

HOLE SUMMARY

HOLE	PAR	EAGLES	BIRDIES	PARS	BOGEYS	D. BOGEYS	HIGHER	RANK	AVERAGE
1	3	0	15	44	11	0	0	12	2.94
2	4	0	4	54	10	2	0	6	4.14
3	4	0	6	37	23	3	1	3	4.37
4	4	0	10	43	15	2	0	8	4.13
5	3	0	2	46	21	0	1	5	3.31
6	5	4	27	30	8	1	0	18	4.64
7	5	0	23	39	4	3	1	15	4.86
8	4	0	9	45	15	1	0	9	4.11
9	3	0	15	51	4	0	0	17	2.84
OUT	35	4	111	389	111	12	3		35.36
10	4	0	6	52	11	1	0	11	4.10
11	5	1	18	38	11	2	0	13	4.93
12	3	0	3	45	19	1	2	3	3.37
13	4	0	13	51	6	0	0	14	3.90
14	4	0	8	47	14	1	0	9	4.11
15	4	0	6	33	24	6	1	1	4.47
16	4	0	17	47	5	1	0	15	3.86
17	4	0	4	41	18	6	1	2	4.41
18	4	0	11	40	17	2	0	6	4.14
IN	36	1	86	394	125	20	4		37.30
TOTAL	71	5	197	783	236	32	7		72.66

Players Below Par	17
Players At Par	11
Players Above Par	42

WEATHER

Temperature: low 14°C, high 21°C.
Westerly breeze.

LOW SCORES

Low First Nine	Davis Love III	30
Low Second Nine	Kevin Sutherland	33
	Mikko Ilonen	33
Low Round	Bob Estes	66
	Mikko Ilonen	66

CHAMPIONSHIP HOLE SUMMARY

HOLE	PAR	YARDS	EAGLES	BIRDIES	PARS	BOGEYS	D.BOGEYS	HIGHER	RANK	AVERAGE
1	3	206	0	41	319	85	4	1	10	3.12
2	4	438	0	61	307	73	8	1	11	4.07
3	4	458	0	28	257	125	35	5	2	4.40
4	4	392	0	51	288	99	12	0	8	4.16
5	3	212	1	30	300	112	4	3	6	3.22
6	5	494	14	205	196	29	6	0	18	4.57
7	5	557	9	183	200	37	13	8	17	4.75
8	4	419	0	60	280	96	13	1	9	4.15
9	3	164	0	96	298	51	3	2	14	2.93
OUT	35	3340	24	755	2445	707	98	21		35.37
10	4	335	0	75	312	57	6	0	12	3.99
11	5	542	6	160	213	57	10	4	16	4.82
12	3	198	0	28	286	127	6	3	4	3.27
13	4	342	3	96	301	43	7	0	15	3.90
14	4	445	1	53	279	103	13	1	7	4.17
15	4	465	0	28	243	143	28	8	1	4.44
16	4	359	0	79	307	56	7	1	12	3.99
17	4	467	0	26	265	135	19	5	3	4.36
18	4	412	0	54	259	114	21	2	5	4.24
IN	36	3565	10	599	2465	835	117	24		37.17
TOTAL	71	6905	34	1354	4910	1542	215	45		72.55

	FIRST ROUND	SECOND ROUND	THIRD ROUND	FOURTH ROUND	TOTAL
Players Below Par	33	47	25	17	122
Players At Par	18	20	9	11	58
Players Above Par	105	87	36	42	270

RELATIVE DIFFICULTY OF HOLES

HOLE	PAR	YARDS	FIRST ROUND	SECOND ROUND	THIRD ROUND	FOURTH ROUND	OVERALL RANK
1	3	206	9	6	8	12	10
2	4	438	14	9	10	6	11
3	4	458	2	1	1	3	2
4	4	392	8	5	8	8	6
5	3	212	5	11	6	5	6
6	5	494	18	18	18	18	18
7	5	557	17	17	17	15	17
8	4	419	10	8	3	9	9
9	3	164	12	14	15	17	14
10	4	335	12	13	13	11	12
11	5	542	16	16	16	13	16
12	3	198	3	7	7	3	4
13	4	342	15	15	13	14	15
14	4	445	4	9	12	9	7
15	4	465	1	3	2	1	1
16	4	359	11	12	11	15	12
17	4	467	6	1	3	2	3
18	4	412	7	4	5	6	5

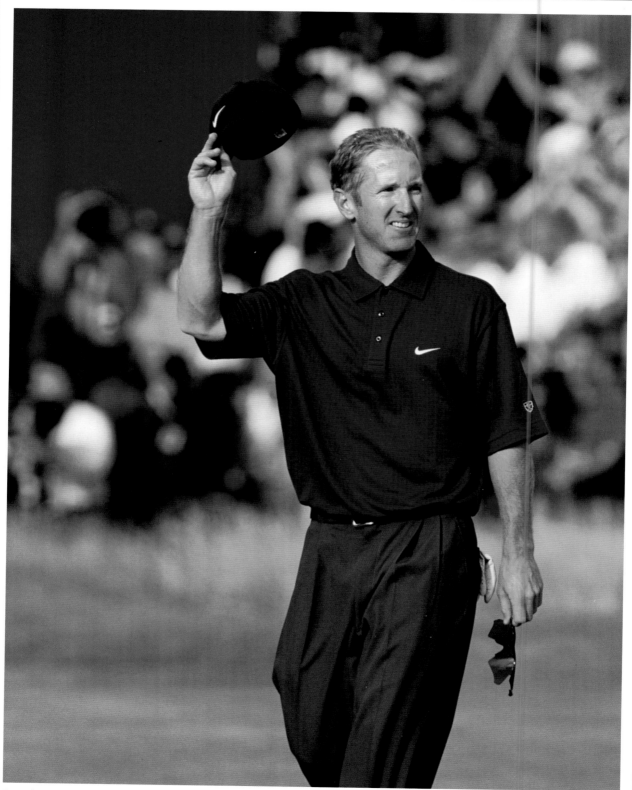

David Duval removed his hat and sunglasses to acknowledge the cheers for his three-stroke victory.

COMMENTARY

ONE YEAR LATER

BY JOHN HOPKINS

Two aeroplane journeys 12 months apart summed up the difference between the David Duval of July 2000 and the David Duval of July 2001. Same man, same month, similar destination, route, and mode of transport, but wildly differing feelings.

What must Duval have been thinking in July last year when he hitched a ride back to the United States on Tiger Woods' private aeroplane? Duval had been a close witness to Woods' triumph in the Open Championship at St Andrews because he had played alongside Tiger. To see Woods pull away over the inward nine holes of the Old Course must have been hard for Duval to bear. Suffering from a sore back, he had tangled with the Road Hole bunker and taken an 8. It was no consolation, as they walked off the 17th green, that Woods put a caring arm around his friend's shoulder. On Woods' aeroplane home Duval must have felt like Banquo's ghost at the feast in Macbeth.

How different that was from the journey that began on the Sunday evening this year, when a small group including Duval, now the Open champion, and Julie, his girl-friend, flew to Toronto where Duval was to compete in a skins game with Sergio Garcia, Mike Weir, and Vijay Singh. A year earlier he had only his own thoughts and it takes little imagination to think he spent a lot of time staring out of a window wondering when his day would come. Now it has. Last year's Open unquestionably belonged to Woods, but this year's belonged to Duval.

His last two rounds in the 130th Open were 65 and 67, a combined 10 under par, which represents very good scoring over such a difficult course, even if the prevailing wind, which makes the last five holes among the most feared finishing stretch in golf, was not blowing. In all Duval took 274 strokes over four rounds and the one that counted the most came on the 15th hole on Sunday.

It was a six iron that travelled 210 yards out of the thick rough on the left of the fairway of a hole that measures 465 yards. It fizzed off the clubface with such a distinctive noise that David Pepper, the rules official who was walking with this match, was quite taken aback. "If you'd been playing someone who hit a ball that made that sound, you'd know you were in trouble," Pepper said. "It was a whizzer."

There has never been any doubt of Duval's ability to hit whizzers. He has been booted and spurred for greatness in golf. The game is in his blood, his father and uncle both being professionals. David and Bob, his father, created history by winning tournaments on the same day in 1999—David, The Players Championship, his father, the Emerald Coast Classic on the Senior PGA Tour.

On the Saturday night after the third round, Duval telephoned his father and the two men talked. "We said that we were going to drink cognac out of the claret jug when he gets home," Bob Duval said on Sunday after watching his son's victory. "I watched him all day Saturday and his swing looked as though it was in the right position. He looked calm from the beginning. I can tell when he gets frustrated and there was no sign of that today."

It's a funny thing to say (and probably a facile thing to say, if the truth be told), but Duval has always had trouble with the Press with words that end in "-ion", words such as frustration, emotion, conversation. He can wrestle with the simplest inquiry as if it were the last question on "Who Wants To Be A Millionaire?" The top button of his golf shirt is always buttoned up, as his mouth is on occasions. He wears dark glasses on the golf course for an eye condition, but they encourage his inscrutability, and perhaps they help him keep his emotions in check, because he knows that people cannot really

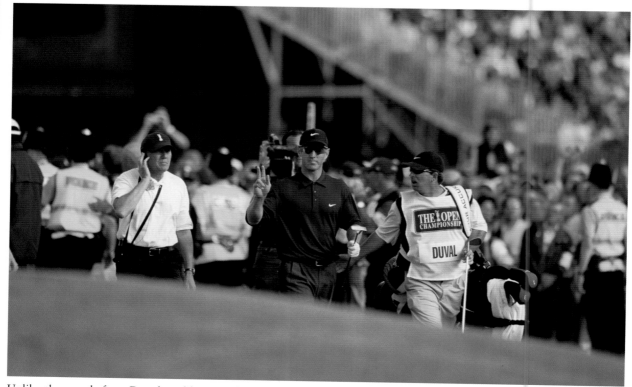

Unlike the year before, Duval could savour his walk along the 18th hole with the crowd sweeping in behind him.

tell what he is thinking because they cannot see his face. If the eyes are the windows of the soul, then hide them and you conceal the soul. That's right, isn't it?

There are reasons why Duval is the way he is. His older brother Brent died of aplastic anaemia when David was nine. It took time for David to come to terms with this, since he had donated some of his bone marrow to Brent and for a while it looked as though it had worked. There is a harrowing story that soon after David heard his brother had died, he burst out, "I killed him." Duval's recovery from this trauma was not helped when his parents, disunited by grief, divorced. Little wonder that he sought refuge on a golf course where he could be alone with his thoughts, his ideals, his dreams.

In a magazine article written about Duval in 1999, there is an evocative passage. "The boy loved to golf alone in fog. No one could see him. He could see no one. It was as if the sky were colluding with him, lowering a grey curtain between him and the world."

Compounding any difficulties that Duval was perceived to have was the fact that, try as he might, he could not get his hands on a major championship. "I have had my chances," Duval admitted. "I had several tries to win on tour before I won and then I've

had several chances to win a major. In 1998 I had a two-stroke lead going into the last round of the Masters. People have written that I have had an arm in a green jacket in the past and it hasn't worked out. They did not write it in a mean way. I was just so close."

Yet, in the aftermath of his triumph this year, there were signs that the man who is portrayed as being slightly troubled, ill at ease in many situations, showed a candour and grace that was striking in one who had hitherto seemed tongue-tied and, as a result, ungraceful. It had probably been there all along. It was just that it only began to emerge in the minutes after his victory, as the crowds began to melt away on the sunlit evening of 22 July 2001.

This, at any rate, is the view of a man who knows Duval well. Puggy Blackmon first came across Duval when he was the head professional at a club in Jacksonville. When he moved to Georgia Institute of Technology (generally known in the United States as Georgia Tech) to become the head golf coach, Blackmon kept an eye on Duval and, in time, was pleased when Duval arrived at the university and became a member of the golf team.

"David was struggling with family life," Blackmon recalled. "His parents had lost a son, which had a

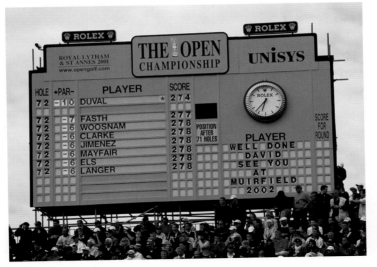

pretty major impact, causing their family to fragment. He came to us and found a fairly normal family and just became a part of it. I think he enjoyed the situation.

"He thought differently to most players I've dealt with. To a coach, David is a once-in-a-lifetime kind of player up there with Tiger Woods, Jack Nicklaus, Ben Hogan. There's not many of them around and it was obvious from the beginning that he was extremely focused on where he wanted to go and the fact that he was going to get there.

"From a golf standpoint, he may have been 17 calendar-wise but he was 25 as a player. At that point he was far more mature as a golfer than the people around him, but socially he was less than 17. The social side had to catch up with the golf side and that is what has happened."

Perhaps the two sides of Duval's character finally met in public this July afternoon in Lancashire.

"I think the history is what's so humbling," Duval said. "What happened is starting to sink in. You grow up with it (the Open). You grow up loving golf as I do. You are aware of the four (major championships). I think that we all recognise that The Players Championship is—you might not want to call it a major, but it is right in the mix somewhere.

"I remember getting up and watching it (the Open) on television. It came on early in the morning back home and in watching it I realised what different golf it was than I was used to. The places, courses, looked different. The atmosphere looked different. Dust and grass flying. You did not see anybody having to carry it over lakes and force carries over bunkers. The Open is different. I loved it when I first came over in 1995. I was lucky that my first Open was at St Andrews. I got a nice taste of Scottish golf the week before at Carnoustie.

"This championship is different from the other majors. In this one I find that when you play a golf course like this one or like Carnoustie, if you make any small mistake it is compounded. There are no ifs and buts. You can't play out of all the bunkers and you can't play much out of the rough unless you get lucky. The added pressure of knowing you really can't mis-hit shots, that you have to hit all of them just right, makes it much more difficult."

Someone once talked of the seven ages of man. There have been three ages of David Duval, his childhood, the tense years of adolescence, and now the time when he is approaching his full and rightful pomp. Holding the claret jug at Royal Lytham and St Annes, he gave about as gracious and winning a speech as it would be possible to give, talking of his first visits to Britain and of the feelings of warmth he held towards those who watched golf in Britain and the feelings he felt they generated towards him.

I have covered 25 Opens and therefore listened to 25 post-round Press conferences by the new champion in which he tries to explain his feelings, to position himself in the game, to outline his emotions, at a time when he is so excited he often cannot express himself as clearly as he would like. I cannot remember the new champion leaving as distinct an impression as Duval, who seemed to have changed in character in the few hours since we had last talked to him. His wise words were humble, engaging, and sensible, and all the more meaningful for that.

"You know what, it is a silly old game," Duval said, and there isn't a golfer in the world who does not know exactly what Duval meant. "I was just trying to hit it solid and move it forward. Then I was going to hit it again and I was going to count on making putts. It sounds stupid, but I found myself thinking at times it is funny how much is made about it, because we are playing a game. At times I've made it a lot bigger than it is, too. Maybe that is some of the reason I felt so good today. I finally realised it is just a game."

Tony Jacklin (1969)

Gary Player (1959, 1968, 1974)

Sandy Lyle (1985)

Bob Charles (1963)

Mark Calcavecchia (1989)

Seve Ballesteros (1979, 1984, 1988)

Tom Watson (1975, 1977, 1980, 1982, 1983)

Nick Faldo (1987, 1990, 1992)

THE OPEN CHAMPIONSHIP

YEAR	CHAMPION	SCORE	MARGIN	RUNNERS-UP	VENUE
1860	Willie Park	174	2	Tom Morris Snr	Prestwick
1861	Tom Morris Snr	163	4	Willie Park	Prestwick
1862	Tom Morris Snr	163	13	Willie Park	Prestwick
1863	Willie Park	168	2	Tom Morris Snr	Prestwick
1864	Tom Morris Snr	167	2	Andrew Strath	Prestwick
1865	Andrew Strath	162	2	Willie Park	Prestwick
1866	Willie Park	169	2	David Park	Prestwick
1867	Tom Morris Snr	170	2	Willie Park	Prestwick
1868	Tom Morris Jnr	157	2	Robert Andrew	Prestwick
1869	Tom Morris Jnr	154	3	Tom Morris Snr	Prestwick
1870	Tom Morris Jnr	149	12	Bob Kirk, David Strath	Prestwick
1871	*No Competition*				
1872	Tom Morris Jnr	166	3	David Strath	Prestwick
1873	Tom Kidd	179	1	Jamie Anderson	St Andrews
1874	Mungo Park	159	2	Tom Morris Jnr	Musselburgh
1875	Willie Park	166	2	Bob Martin	Prestwick
1876	Bob Martin	176	—	David Strath	St Andrews
				(Martin was awarded the title when Strath refused to play-off)	
1877	Jamie Anderson	160	2	Bob Pringle	Musselburgh
1878	Jamie Anderson	157	2	Bob Kirk	Prestwick
1879	Jamie Anderson	169	3	James Allan, Andrew Kirkaldy	St Andrews
1880	Bob Ferguson	162	5	Peter Paxton	Musselburgh
1881	Bob Ferguson	170	3	Jamie Anderson	Prestwick
1882	Bob Ferguson	171	3	Willie Fernie	St Andrews
1883	Willie Fernie	159	Play-off	Bob Ferguson	Musselburgh
1884	Jack Simpson	160	4	David Rollan, Willie Fernie	Prestwick
1885	Bob Martin	171	1	Archie Simpson	St Andrews
1886	David Brown	157	2	Willie Campbell	Musselburgh
1887	Willie Park Jnr	161	1	Bob Martin	Prestwick
1888	Jack Burns	171	1	David Anderson Jnr, Ben Sayers	St Andrews
1889	Willie Park Jnr	155	Play-off	Andrew Kirkaldy	Musselburgh
1890	*John Ball	164	3	Willie Fernie, Archie Simpson	Prestwick
1891	Hugh Kirkaldy	166	2	Willie Fernie, Andrew Kirkaldy	St Andrews
(From 1892 the competition was extended to 72 holes)					
1892	*Harold Hilton	305	3	*John Ball Jnr, James Kirkaldy, Sandy Herd	Muirfield
1893	Willie Auchterlonie	322	2	*Johnny Laidlay	Prestwick
1894	J.H. Taylor	326	5	Douglas Rolland	Sandwich
1895	J.H. Taylor	322	4	Sandy Herd	St Andrews
1896	Harry Vardon	316	Play-off	J.H. Taylor	Muirfield

YEAR	CHAMPION	SCORE	MARGIN	RUNNERS-UP	VENUE
1897	*Harold H. Hilton	314	1	James Braid	Hoylake
1898	Harry Vardon	307	1	Willie Park	Prestwick
1899	Harry Vardon	310	5	Jack White	Sandwich
1900	J.H. Taylor	309	8	Harry Vardon	St Andrews
1901	James Braid	309	3	Harry Vardon	Muirfield
1902	Sandy Herd	307	1	Harry Vardon, James Braid	Hoylake
1903	Harry Vardon	300	6	Tom Vardon	Prestwick
1904	Jack White	296	1	James Braid, J.H. Taylor	Sandwich
1905	James Braid	318	5	J.H. Taylor, R. Jones	St Andrews
1906	James Braid	300	4	J.H. Taylor	Muirfield
1907	Arnaud Massy	312	2	J.H. Taylor	Hoylake
1908	James Braid	291	8	Tom Ball	Prestwick
1909	J.H. Taylor	295	4	James Braid	Deal
1910	James Braid	299	4	Sandy Herd	St Andrews
1911	Harry Vardon	303	Play-off	Arnaud Massy	Sandwich
1912	Ted Ray	295	4	Harry Vardon	Muirfield
1913	J.H. Taylor	304	8	Ted Ray	Hoylake
1914	Harry Vardon	306	3	J.H. Taylor	Prestwick

1915-1919 No Championship

YEAR	CHAMPION	SCORE	MARGIN	RUNNERS-UP	VENUE
1920	George Duncan	303	2	Sandy Herd	Deal
1921	Jock Hutchison	296	Play-off	*Roger Wethered	St Andrews
1922	Walter Hagen	300	1	George Duncan, Jim Barnes	Sandwich
1923	Arthur G. Havers	295	1	Walter Hagen	Troon
1924	Walter Hagen	301	1	Ernest Whitcombe	Hoylake
1925	Jim Barnes	300	1	Archie Compston, Ted Ray	Prestwick
1926	*Robert T. Jones Jnr	291	2	Al Watrous	Royal Lytham
1927	*Robert T. Jones Jnr	285	6	Aubrey Boomer, Fred Robson	St Andrews
1928	Walter Hagen	292	2	Gene Sarazen	Sandwich
1929	Walter Hagen	292	6	John Farrell	Muirfield
1930	*Robert T. Jones Jnr	291	2	Leo Diegel, Macdonald Smith	Hoylake
1931	Tommy Armour	296	1	Jose Jurado	Carnoustie
1932	Gene Sarazen	283	5	Macdonald Smith	Prince's
1933	Densmore Shute	292	Play-off	Craig Wood	St Andrews
1934	Henry Cotton	283	5	Sid Brews	Sandwich
1935	Alf Perry	283	4	Alf Padgham	Muirfield
1936	Alf Padgham	287	1	Jimmy Adams	Hoylake
1937	Henry Cotton	290	2	Reg Whitcombe	Carnoustie
1938	Reg Whitcombe	295	2	Jimmy Adams	Sandwich
1939	Richard Burton	290	2	Johnny Bulla	St Andrews

1940-1945 No Championship

YEAR	CHAMPION	SCORE	MARGIN	RUNNERS-UP	VENUE
1946	Sam Snead	290	4	Bobby Locke, Johnny Bulla	St Andrews
1947	Fred Daly	293	1	Reg Horne, *Frank Stranahan	Hoylake
1948	Henry Cotton	284	5	Fred Daly	Muirfield
1949	Bobby Locke	283	Play-off	Harry Bradshaw	Sandwich
1950	Bobby Locke	279	2	Roberto de Vicenzo	Troon
1951	Max Faulkner	285	2	Tony Cerda	Royal Portrush
1952	Bobby Locke	287	1	Peter Thomson	Royal Lytham
1953	Ben Hogan	282	4	*Frank Stranahan, Dai Rees, Peter Thomson, Tony Cerda	Carnoustie
1954	Peter Thomson	283	1	Sid Scott, Dai Rees, Bobby Locke	Royal Birkdale
1955	Peter Thomson	281	2	Johnny Fallon	St Andrews
1956	Peter Thomson	286	3	Flory van Donck	Hoylake
1957	Bobby Locke	279	3	Peter Thomson	St Andrews
1958	Peter Thomson	278	Play-off	David Thomas	Royal Lytham
1959	Gary Player	284	2	Flory van Donck, Fred Bullock	Muirfield
1960	Kel Nagle	278	1	Arnold Palmer	St Andrews

YEAR	CHAMPION	SCORE	MARGIN	RUNNERS-UP	VENUE
1961	Arnold Palmer	284	1	Dai Rees	Royal Birkdale
1962	Arnold Palmer	276	6	Kel Nagle	Troon
1963	Bob Charles	277	Play-off	Phil Rodgers	Royal Lytham
1964	Tony Lema	279	5	Jack Nicklaus	St Andrews
1965	Peter Thomson	285	2	Christy O'Connor, Brian Huggett	Royal Birkdale
1966	Jack Nicklaus	282	1	David Thomas, Doug Sanders	Muirfield
1967	Roberto de Vicenzo	278	2	Jack Nicklaus	Hoylake
1968	Gary Player	289	2	Jack Nicklaus, Bob Charles	Carnoustie
1969	Tony Jacklin	280	2	Bob Charles	Royal Lytham
1970	Jack Nicklaus	283	Play-off	Doug Sanders	St Andrews
1971	Lee Trevino	278	1	Lu Liang Huan	Royal Birkdale
1972	Lee Trevino	278	1	Jack Nicklaus	Muirfield
1973	Tom Weiskopf	276	3	Neil Coles, Johnny Miller	Troon
1974	Gary Player	282	4	Peter Oosterhuis	Royal Lytham
1975	Tom Watson	279	Play-off	Jack Newton	Carnoustie
1976	Johnny Miller	279	6	Jack Nicklaus, Severiano Ballesteros	Royal Birkdale
1977	Tom Watson	268	1	Jack Nicklaus	Turnberry
1978	Jack Nicklaus	281	2	Simon Owen, Ben Crenshaw, Raymond Floyd, Tom Kite	St Andrews
1979	Severiano Ballesteros	283	3	Jack Nicklaus, Ben Crenshaw	Royal Lytham
1980	Tom Watson	271	4	Lee Trevino	Muirfield
1981	Bill Rogers	276	4	Bernhard Langer	Sandwich
1982	Tom Watson	284	1	Peter Oosterhuis, Nick Price	Troon
1983	Tom Watson	275	1	Hale Irwin, Andy Bean	Royal Birkdale
1984	Severiano Ballesteros	276	2	Bernhard Langer, Tom Watson	St Andrews
1985	Sandy Lyle	282	1	Payne Stewart	Sandwich
1986	Greg Norman	280	5	Gordon J. Brand	Turnberry
1987	Nick Faldo	279	1	Rodger Davis, Paul Azinger	Muirfield
1988	Severiano Ballesteros	273	2	Nick Price	Royal Lytham
1989	Mark Calcavecchia	275	Play-off	Greg Norman, Wayne Grady	Royal Troon
1990	Nick Faldo	270	5	Mark McNulty, Payne Stewart	St Andrews
1991	Ian Baker-Finch	272	2	Mike Harwood	Royal Birkdale
1992	Nick Faldo	272	1	John Cook	Muirfield
1993	Greg Norman	267	2	Nick Faldo	Sandwich
1994	Nick Price	268	1	Jesper Parnevik	Turnberry
1995	John Daly	282	Play-off	Costantino Rocca	St Andrews
1996	Tom Lehman	271	2	Mark McCumber, Ernie Els	Royal Lytham
1997	Justin Leonard	272	3	Jesper Parnevik, Darren Clarke	Royal Troon
1998	Mark O'Meara	280	Play-off	Brian Watts	Royal Birkdale
1999	Paul Lawrie	290	Play-off	Justin Leonard, Jean Van de Velde	Carnoustie
2000	Tiger Woods	269	8	Ernie Els, Thomas Bjorn	St Andrews
2001	David Duval	274	3	Niclas Fasth	Royal Lytham

*Denotes amateurs

Tiger Woods (2000)

Paul Lawrie (1999)

Justin Leonard (1997)

John Daly (1995)

Nick Price (1994)

Tom Lehman (1996)

Mark O'Meara (1998)

THE OPEN CHAMPIONSHIP

MOST VICTORIES
6, Harry Vardon, 1896-98-99-1903-11-14
5, James Braid, 1901-05-06-08-10; J.H. Taylor, 1894-95-1900-09-13; Peter Thomson, 1954-55-56-58-65; Tom Watson, 1975-77-80-82-83

MOST TIMES RUNNER-UP OR JOINT RUNNER-UP
7, Jack Nicklaus, 1964-67-68-72-76-77-79
6, J.H. Taylor, 1896-1904-05-06-07-14

OLDEST WINNER
Old Tom Morris, 46 years 99 days, 1867
Roberto de Vicenzo, 44 years 93 days, 1967

YOUNGEST WINNER
Young Tom Morris, 17 years 5 months 8 days, 1868
Willie Auchterlonie, 21 years 24 days, 1893
Severiano Ballesteros, 22 years 3 months 12 days, 1979

YOUNGEST AND OLDEST COMPETITOR
Young Tom Morris, 14 years 4 months 4 days, 1865
Gene Sarazen, 71 years 4 months 13 days, 1973

BIGGEST MARGIN OF VICTORY
13 strokes, Old Tom Morris, 1862
12 strokes, Young Tom Morris, 1870
8 strokes, J.H. Taylor, 1900 and 1913; James Braid, 1908; Tiger Woods, 2000

LOWEST WINNING AGGREGATES
267 (66, 68, 69, 64), Greg Norman, Royal St George's, 1993
268 (68, 70, 65, 65), Tom Watson, Turnberry, 1977; (69, 66, 67, 66), Nick Price, Turnberry, 1994
269 (67, 66, 67, 69), Tiger Woods, St Andrews, 2000

LOWEST AGGREGATE IN RELATION TO PAR
269 (19 under par), Tiger Woods, St Andrews, 2000

LOWEST AGGREGATES BY RUNNER-UP
269 (68, 70, 65, 66), Jack Nicklaus, Turnberry, 1977; (69, 63, 70, 67), Nick Faldo, Royal St George's, 1993; (68, 66, 68, 67), Jesper Parnevik, Turnberry, 1994

LOWEST AGGREGATES BY AN AMATEUR
281 (68, 72, 70, 71), Iain Pyman, Royal St George's, 1993; (75, 66, 70, 70), Tiger Woods, Royal Lytham, 1996

LOWEST INDIVIDUAL ROUND
63, Mark Hayes, second round, Turnberry, 1977; Isao Aoki, third round, Muirfield, 1980; Greg Norman, second round, Turnberry, 1986; Paul Broadhurst, third round, St Andrews, 1990; Jodie Mudd, fourth round, Royal Birkdale, 1991; Nick Faldo, second round, and Payne Stewart, fourth round, Royal St George's, 1993

LOWEST INDIVIDUAL ROUND BY AN AMATEUR
66, Frank Stranahan, fourth round, Troon, 1950; Tiger Woods, second round, Royal Lytham, 1996; Justin Rose, second round, Royal Birkdale, 1998

LOWEST FIRST ROUND
64, Craig Stadler, Royal Birkdale, 1983; Christy O'Connor Jnr., Royal St George's, 1985; Rodger Davis, Muirfield, 1987; Raymond Floyd and Steve Pate, Muirfield, 1992

LOWEST SECOND ROUND
63, Mark Hayes, Turnberry, 1977; Greg Norman, Turnberry, 1986; Nick Faldo, Royal St George's, 1993

LOWEST THIRD ROUND
63, Isao Aoki, Muirfield, 1980; Paul Broadhurst, St Andrews, 1990

LOWEST FOURTH ROUND
63, Jodie Mudd, Royal Birkdale, 1991; Payne Stewart, Royal St George's, 1993

LOWEST FIRST 36 HOLES
130 (66, 64), Nick Faldo, Muirfield, 1992

LOWEST SECOND 36 HOLES
130 (65, 65), Tom Watson, Turnberry, 1977; (64, 66), Ian Baker-Finch, Royal Birkdale, 1991; (66, 64), Anders Forsbrand, Turnberry, 1994

LOWEST FIRST 54 HOLES
198 (67, 67, 64), Tom Lehman, Royal Lytham, 1996

LOWEST FINAL 54 HOLES
199 (66, 67, 66), Nick Price, Turnberry, 1994

LOWEST 9 HOLES
28, Denis Durnian, first 9, Royal Birkdale, 1983
29, Peter Thomson and Tom Haliburton, first 9, Royal Lytham, 1958; Tony Jacklin, first 9, St Andrews, 1970; Bill Longmuir, first 9, Royal Lytham, 1979; David J. Russell, first 9, Royal Lytham, 1988; Ian Baker-Finch and Paul Broadhurst, first 9, St Andrews, 1990; Ian Baker-Finch, first 9, Royal Birkdale, 1991; Paul McGinley, first 9, Royal Lytham, 1996

BIGGEST SPAN BETWEEN FIRST AND LAST VICTORIES
19 years, J.H. Taylor, 1894-1913
18 years, Harry Vardon, 1896-1914
15 years, Gary Player, 1959-74
14 years, Henry Cotton, 1934-48

SUCCESSIVE VICTORIES
4, Young Tom Morris, 1868-72. No championship in 1871
3, Jamie Anderson, 1877-79; Bob Ferguson, 1880-82, Peter Thomson, 1954-56
2, Old Tom Morris, 1861-62; J.H. Taylor, 1894-95; Harry Vardon, 1898-99; James Braid, 1905-06; Bobby Jones, 1926-27; Walter Hagen, 1928-29; Bobby Locke, 1949-50; Arnold Palmer, 1961-62; Lee Trevino, 1971-72; Tom Watson, 1982-83

VICTORIES BY AMATEURS
3, Bobby Jones, 1926-27-30
2, Harold Hilton, 1892-97
1, John Ball, 1890
Roger Wethered lost a play-off in 1921

HIGHEST NUMBER OF TOP FIVE FINISHES
16, J.H. Taylor, Jack Nicklaus
15, Harry Vardon, James Braid

HIGHEST NUMBER OF ROUNDS UNDER 70
33, Jack Nicklaus, Nick Faldo
27, Tom Watson
23, Greg Norman
22, Nick Price
21, Lee Trevino, Severiano Ballesteros

OUTRIGHT LEADER AFTER EVERY ROUND
Willie Auchterlonie, 1893; J.H. Taylor, 1894 and 1900; James Braid, 1908; Ted Ray, 1912; Bobby Jones, 1927; Gene Sarazen, 1932; Henry Cotton, 1934; Tom Weiskopf, 1973

RECORD LEADS (SINCE 1892)
After 18 holes:
4 strokes, James Braid, 1908; Bobby Jones, 1927; Henry Cotton, 1934; Christy O'Connor Jnr., 1985
After 36 holes:
9 strokes, Henry Cotton, 1934
After 54 holes:
10 strokes, Henry Cotton, 1934
7 strokes, Tony Lema, 1964

CHAMPIONS WITH EACH ROUND LOWER THAN PREVIOUS ONE
Jack White, 1904, Sandwich, (80, 75, 72, 69)
James Braid, 1906, Muirfield, (77, 76, 74, 73)
Ben Hogan, 1953, Carnoustie, (73, 71, 70, 68)
Gary Player, 1959, Muirfield, (75, 71, 70, 68)

CHAMPION WITH FOUR ROUNDS THE SAME
Densmore Shute, 1933, St Andrews, (73, 73, 73, 73) (excluding the play-off)

BIGGEST VARIATION BETWEEN ROUNDS OF A CHAMPION
14 strokes, Henry Cotton, 1934, second round 65, fourth round 79
11 strokes, Jack White, 1904, first round 80, fourth round 69; Greg Norman, 1986, first round 74, second round 63, third round 74

BIGGEST VARIATION BETWEEN TWO ROUNDS
18 strokes, A. Tingey Jnr., 1923, first round 94, second round 76
17 strokes, Jack Nicklaus, 1981, first round 83, second round 66; Ian Baker-Finch, 1986, first round 86, second round 69

BEST COMEBACK BY CHAMPIONS
After 18 holes:
Harry Vardon, 1896, 11 strokes behind the leader
After 36 holes:
George Duncan, 1920, 13 strokes behind the leader
After 54 holes:
Paul Lawrie, 1999, 10 strokes behind the leader

CHAMPIONS WITH FOUR ROUNDS UNDER 70
Greg Norman, 1993, Royal St George's, (66, 68, 69, 64); Nick Price, 1994, Turnberry, (69, 66, 67, 66); Tiger Woods, 2000, St Andrews, (67, 66, 67, 69)
Of non-champions:
Ernie Els, 1993, Royal St George's, (68, 69, 69, 68); Jesper Parnevik, 1994, Turnberry, (68, 66, 68, 67)

BEST FINISHING ROUND BY A CHAMPION
64, Greg Norman, Royal St George's, 1993
65, Tom Watson, Turnberry, 1977; Severiano Ballesteros, Royal Lytham, 1988; Justin Leonard, Royal Troon, 1997

WORST FINISHING ROUND BY A CHAMPION SINCE 1920
79, Henry Cotton, Sandwich, 1934
78, Reg Whitcombe, Sandwich, 1938
77, Walter Hagen, Hoylake, 1924

WORST OPENING ROUND BY A CHAMPION SINCE 1919
80, George Duncan, Deal, 1920 (he also had a second round of 80)
77, Walter Hagen, Hoylake, 1924

BEST OPENING ROUND BY A CHAMPION
66, Peter Thomson, Royal Lytham, 1958; Nick Faldo, Muirfield, 1992; Greg Norman, Royal St George's, 1993

BIGGEST RECOVERY IN 18 HOLES BY A CHAMPION

George Duncan, Deal, 1920, was 13 strokes behind the leader, Abe Mitchell, after 36 holes and level after 54

MOST APPEARANCES ON FINAL DAY (SINCE 1892)

32, Jack Nicklaus
30, J.H. Taylor
27, Harry Vardon, James Braid
26, Peter Thomson, Gary Player
23, Dai Rees
22, Henry Cotton

CHAMPIONSHIP WITH HIGHEST NUMBER OF ROUNDS UNDER 70

148, Turnberry, 1994

CHAMPIONSHIP SINCE 1946 WITH THE FEWEST ROUNDS UNDER 70

St Andrews, 1946; Hoylake, 1947; Portrush, 1951; Hoylake, 1956; Carnoustie, 1968. All had only two rounds under 70

LONGEST COURSE

Carnoustie, 1999, 7361 yd

COURSES MOST OFTEN USED

St Andrews, 26; Prestwick, 24; Muirfield, 14; Sandwich, 12; Hoylake and Royal Lytham, 10; Royal Birkdale, 8; Royal Troon, 7; Musselburgh and Carnoustie, 6; Turnberry, 3; Deal, 2; Royal Portrush and Prince's, 1

PRIZE MONEY

Year	Total	First Prize
1860	nil	nil
1863	10	nil
1864	16	6
1876	27	10
1889	22	8
1891	28.50	10
1892	110	(Amateur winner)
1893	100	30
1910	125	50
1920	225	75
1927	275	100
1930	400	100
1931	500	100
1946	1,000	150
1949	1,700	300
1953	2,450	500
1954	3,500	750
1955	3,750	1,000
1958	4,850	1,000
1959	5,000	1,000
1960	7,000	1,250
1961	8,500	1,400
1963	8,500	1,500
1965	10,000	1,750
1966	15,000	2,100
1968	20,000	3,000
1969	30,000	4,250
1970	40,000	5,250
1971	45,000	5,500
1972	50,000	5,500
1975	75,000	7,500
1977	100,000	10,000
1978	125,000	12,500
1979	155,000	15,500
1980	200,000	25,000
1982	250,000	32,000
1983	300,000	40,000
1984	451,000	55,000
1985	530,000	65,000
1986	600,000	70,000
1987	650,000	75,000
1988	700,000	80,000
1989	750,000	80,000
1990	825,000	85,000
1991	900,000	90,000
1992	950,000	95,000
1993	1,000,000	100,000
1994	1,100,000	110,000
1995	1,250,000	125,000
1996	1,400,000	200,000
1997	1,600,000	250,000
1998	1,800,000	300,000
1999	2,000,000	350,000
2000	2,750,000	500,000
2001	3,300,000	600,000

ATTENDANCE

Year	Attendance
1962	37,098
1963	24,585
1964	35,954
1965	32,927
1966	40,182
1967	29,880
1968	51,819
1969	46,001
1970	81,593
1971	70,076
1972	84,746
1973	78,810
1974	92,796
1975	85,258
1976	92,021
1977	87,615
1978	125,271
1979	134,501
1980	131,610
1981	111,987
1982	133,299
1983	142,892
1984	193,126
1985	141,619
1986	134,261
1987	139,189
1988	191,334
1989	160,639
1990	208,680
1991	189,435
1992	146,427
1993	141,000
1994	128,000
1995	180,000
1996	171,000
1997	176,000
1998	195,100
1999	157,000
2000	230,000
2001	178,000

THE 130TH OPEN CHAMPIONSHIP

*Denotes amateurs

HOLE		1	2	3	4	5	6	7	8	9	10	11	12	13	14	15	16	17	18	
PAR		3	4	4	4	3	5	5	4	3	4	5	3	4	4	4	4	4	4	TOTAL
David Duval	Round 1	3	4	4	5	4	4	4	4	2	3	4	3	4	5	4	4	4	4	69
USA	Round 2	3	4	4	3	3	4	5	4	3	6	4	4	5	4	4	4	4	5	73
£600,000	Round 3	3	3	4	4	3	5	4	3	3	3	4	3	3	3	5	4	4	4	65
	Round 4	3	4	3	4	3	4	4	4	3	4	4	3	4	4	4	4	4	4	67-274
Niclas Fasth	Round 1	3	4	4	4	4	4	5	3	3	4	4	4	5	4	4	3	4	3	69
Sweden	Round 2	3	3	4	4	3	4	4	4	3	4	5	3	5	4	4	4	3	5	69
£360,000	Round 3	3	4	5	4	3	4	5	4	3	4	5	3	4	4	5	4	4	4	72
	Round 4	2	4	3	4	3	4	4	4	3	4	4	3	4	5	4	4	4	4	67-277
Ernie Els	Round 1	4	4	5	4	3	4	6	4	2	4	5	4	4	4	3	4	4	3	71
South Africa	Round 2	3	4	4	4	3	5	5	4	3	4	4	3	4	4	5	4	5	3	71
£141,667	Round 3	3	5	4	3	3	4	4	4	2	4	5	3	3	4	4	4	4	3	67
	Round 4	3	4	4	5	3	5	5	4	2	4	5	3	4	3	4	4	4	3	69-278
Darren Clarke	Round 1	5	4	4	3	3	5	5	4	3	3	5	4	4	4	4	4	3	3	70
N. Ireland	Round 2	3	4	3	4	3	4	4	4	3	5	4	3	3	4	5	5	4	4	69
£141,667	Round 3	3	3	4	4	2	4	4	4	4	4	5	3	4	4	4	4	4	5	69
	Round 4	3	4	5	4	3	3	5	4	3	4	4	3	4	4	4	3	6	4	70-278
Billy Mayfair	Round 1	3	4	5	3	3	4	4	4	3	4	4	4	4	4	4	4	4	4	69
USA	Round 2	3	4	5	4	4	4	4	5	2	4	4	3	4	4	5	5	5	3	72
£141,667	Round 3	3	4	4	4	3	4	5	4	2	4	5	3	4	4	3	4	4	3	67
	Round 4	3	4	4	4	3	4	4	4	3	4	6	3	4	4	4	4	4	4	70-278
Miguel Angel Jimenez	Round 1	3	4	5	5	3	4	4	5	3	4	4	3	4	4	4	3	4	3	69
Spain	Round 2	4	4	4	4	6	4	4	4	3	3	5	2	4	4	4	4	5	5	72
£141,667	Round 3	3	3	4	4	3	4	4	4	3	4	4	3	3	5	5	4	4	4	67
	Round 4	2	5	4	4	3	4	4	5	3	4	4	3	3	5	5	4	4	4	70-278
Ian Woosnam	Round 1	3	3	5	4	3	5	5	4	3	3	6	4	4	4	5	3	4	4	72
Wales	Round 2	3	4	5	4	3	4	4	4	3	4	4	3	3	4	4	4	4	4	68
£141,667	Round 3	3	4	4	4	3	4	5	5	4	3	4	3	3	4	3	5	3	4	67
	Round 4	4	4	5	5	3	3	5	4	3	4	4	3	3	4	5	3	5	4	71-278
Bernhard Langer	Round 1	4	3	4	5	3	5	4	5	3	5	5	3	3	3	4	4	4	4	71
Germany	Round 2	3	3	4	4	5	5	5	5	2	5	4	2	4	4	4	4	4	4	69
£141,667	Round 3	2	4	5	4	3	4	4	4	3	3	4	3	4	3	5	3	4	4	67
	Round 4	3	4	4	4	3	5	5	4	3	4	6	3	4	3	4	3	4	4	71-278

HOLE		1	2	3	4	5	6	7	8	9	10	11	12	13	14	15	16	17	18	TOTAL
PAR		3	4	4	4	3	5	5	4	3	4	5	3	4	4	4	4	4	4	TOTAL
Mikko Ilonen Finland £63,750	Round 1	2	4	3	4	3	5	5	4	2	4	5	3	3	5	4	3	5	4	68
	Round 2	3	6	4	4	3	4	4	4	3	5	8	3	4	4	4	3	4	5	75
	Round 3	4	4	4	4	3	5	5	4	3	4	4	3	4	4	4	5	3	3	70
	Round 4	3	4	4	4	2	4	5	5	2	3	5	2	3	4	4	4	4	4	66-279
Kevin Sutherland USA £63,750	Round 1	4	3	4	6	4	5	4	3	3	4	6	3	4	6	4	4	4	4	75
	Round 2	3	4	5	4	3	4	4	3	3	4	5	3	4	5	4	4	4	4	69
	Round 3	3	4	4	3	3	5	5	4	2	4	5	3	4	3	4	4	4	3	68
	Round 4	2	4	4	5	4	5	4	4	2	4	4	3	4	4	3	4	4	3	67-279
Sergio Garcia Spain £63,750	Round 1	3	4	4	5	3	4	5	4	2	4	4	3	4	4	5	4	4	4	70
	Round 2	4	3	5	3	3	5	5	5	3	4	4	3	4	4	4	4	5	5	72
	Round 3	3	3	4	4	3	5	4	3	3	4	4	4	4	3	4	4	5	3	67
	Round 4	3	4	5	4	3	3	5	4	2	4	5	4	4	4	4	4	4	4	70-279
Jesper Parnevik Sweden £63,750	Round 1	3	4	4	5	2	3	4	4	4	4	5	4	3	4	5	3	4	4	69
	Round 2	2	4	4	4	3	5	4	3	3	4	4	3	4	5	3	4	5	4	68
	Round 3	4	3	4	5	3	4	5	6	2	3	4	2	4	4	4	4	6	4	71
	Round 4	3	4	5	4	4	5	4	4	3	4	5	3	3	4	4	3	4	5	71-279
Vijay Singh Fiji £40,063	Round 1	3	4	4	4	3	6	4	3	2	4	5	3	4	4	5	4	4	4	70
	Round 2	3	4	4	4	4	5	5	4	3	4	5	2	3	4	4	4	4	4	70
	Round 3	3	5	5	4	3	4	6	5	2	3	5	4	3	3	4	3	4	5	71
	Round 4	4	4	4	4	3	3	4	3	3	4	5	3	4	3	4	4	4	6	69-280
Loren Roberts USA £40,063	Round 1	3	4	4	4	4	4	5	4	2	3	4	4	4	4	4	5	4	4	70
	Round 2	3	4	4	5	3	4	5	4	3	4	5	3	4	3	3	4	5	4	70
	Round 3	3	4	4	4	3	4	4	4	3	4	5	3	4	3	3	4	5	4	70
	Round 4	3	4	4	4	3	5	4	4	3	4	6	3	4	5	5	4	3	3	70-280
Des Smyth Ireland £40,063	Round 1	3	5	4	4	2	5	4	5	3	4	5	4	5	4	4	4	6	3	74
	Round 2	4	4	3	5	3	4	3	4	2	3	4	3	4	3	4	4	4	4	65
	Round 3	2	4	5	4	3	4	5	4	2	3	5	3	5	4	4	4	5	4	70
	Round 4	3	4	4	4	4	4	5	4	2	4	5	3	4	5	4	4	4	4	71-280
Billy Andrade USA £40,063	Round 1	3	5	4	4	3	5	5	3	3	3	5	3	4	3	4	4	4	4	69
	Round 2	3	4	4	4	3	4	4	4	3	4	5	3	5	4	4	4	5	3	70
	Round 3	3	4	4	4	4	5	4	3	3	4	6	3	4	2	4	4	4	4	70
	Round 4	3	4	4	4	4	4	5	4	3	4	5	3	3	3	6	4	4	4	71-280
Retief Goosen South Africa £40,063	Round 1	4	4	4	4	4	4	5	3	3	4	4	2	4	5	5	5	6	4	74
	Round 2	3	4	4	3	3	4	4	4	4	4	4	3	4	4	4	3	5	4	68
	Round 3	2	4	4	4	3	4	4	4	3	5	5	2	4	4	4	3	5	4	68
	Round 4	3	4	3	5	3	6	5	4	2	4	5	3	3	3	5	4	4	4	71-280
Colin Montgomerie Scotland £40,063	Round 1	2	3	4	4	4	3	5	3	2	3	5	3	4	5	4	4	4	3	65
	Round 2	3	4	5	4	3	4	5	4	3	4	4	3	3	4	5	4	4	4	70
	Round 3	3	4	4	5	3	5	5	5	3	3	4	3	6	4	4	4	4	4	73
	Round 4	3	4	5	4	4	4	4	4	3	5	5	3	3	4	5	4	4	4	72-280
Raphael Jacquelin France £40,063	Round 1	4	3	4	4	4	5	5	4	2	4	4	3	4	3	4	5	4	4	71
	Round 2	3	4	4	4	3	4	5	3	2	3	5	4	4	4	5	3	4	4	68
	Round 3	4	3	4	4	3	5	4	4	2	3	5	4	4	4	4	4	4	4	69
	Round 4	4	4	4	4	3	5	4	3	4	4	4	3	4	4	4	4	5	4	72-280
Alex Cejka Germany £40,063	Round 1	3	4	4	4	2	4	6	4	3	4	4	3	3	4	5	4	4	4	69
	Round 2	3	4	4	4	3	5	4	4	3	4	5	3	3	3	5	3	4	5	69
	Round 3	3	5	4	4	2	4	4	4	2	3	4	4	4	3	5	5	5	4	69
	Round 4	3	4	5	5	6	4	5	4	3	4	4	4	4	4	4	3	3	4	73-280

HOLE		1	2	3	4	5	6	7	8	9	10	11	12	13	14	15	16	17	18	TOTAL
PAR		3	4	4	4	3	5	5	4	3	4	5	3	4	4	4	4	4	4	TOTAL
Davis Love III USA £32,500	Round 1	4	5	5	4	3	5	4	4	2	4	5	3	4	5	4	4	4	4	73
	Round 2	3	4	3	4	3	5	4	4	3	4	4	3	4	4	3	3	5	4	67
	Round 3	3	4	5	3	3	5	4	6	2	4	6	4	4	3	5	4	5	4	74
	Round 4	3	3	5	3	3	4	4	3	2	4	4	3	5	4	4	4	5	4	67-281
Nick Price Zimbabwe £32,500	Round 1	3	4	5	4	3	4	5	5	2	4	4	4	4	4	5	4	5	4	73
	Round 2	3	3	4	4	2	4	5	4	2	4	6	3	3	3	5	4	4	4	67
	Round 3	3	4	4	4	3	4	4	5	2	4	5	3	3	3	4	4	5	4	68
	Round 4	2	4	5	4	4	5	5	3	3	4	4	3	5	4	5	4	4	5	73-281
Michael Campbell New Zealand £30,500	Round 1	3	4	3	6	3	3	6	3	3	4	5	4	6	3	4	3	4	4	71
	Round 2	3	4	4	4	3	4	4	4	3	5	5	4	4	4	4	4	4	5	72
	Round 3	4	4	4	5	3	5	5	3	2	4	5	3	4	4	4	4	4	4	71
	Round 4	3	4	3	4	3	5	4	3	3	4	4	3	4	4	4	4	5	4	68-282
Greg Owen England £30,500	Round 1	3	4	4	3	3	3	5	4	4	4	5	3	4	4	4	4	4	4	69
	Round 2	2	5	3	4	3	5	5	4	3	4	4	3	3	4	4	4	3	5	68
	Round 3	3	5	4	6	3	5	4	4	2	4	2	3	4	4	5	5	5	5	72
	Round 4	3	6	4	4	3	4	4	4	3	4	5	3	4	5	5	3	4	5	73-282
Bob Estes USA £27,500	Round 1	3	4	4	4	4	4	5	5	3	4	7	3	3	3	5	5	4	4	74
	Round 2	3	4	4	4	3	4	4	4	3	3	4	3	4	5	4	4	4	6	70
	Round 3	3	3	4	4	4	7	4	5	4	4	4	4	3	3	4	4	5	4	73
	Round 4	2	4	3	4	4	5	4	4	2	4	5	3	4	4	3	3	5	3	66-283
Tiger Woods USA £27,500	Round 1	2	4	4	5	3	5	5	4	3	5	5	3	3	5	4	3	4	4	71
	Round 2	3	4	4	4	3	4	4	4	3	4	4	3	4	3	5	4	4	5	68
	Round 3	2	4	4	3	4	4	7	4	3	4	5	3	4	5	4	4	3	3	71
	Round 4	4	4	4	3	2	4	5	4	3	4	5	6	4	4	5	3	3	4	71-283
Eduardo Romero Argentina £27,500	Round 1	3	4	4	3	3	5	4	4	3	4	5	4	5	3	5	3	4	4	70
	Round 2	3	4	5	4	3	5	4	4	2	4	4	3	3	4	4	4	4	4	68
	Round 3	4	4	4	3	3	5	4	4	3	5	6	4	4	4	4	4	4	3	72
	Round 4	3	4	5	4	3	4	5	4	3	4	5	4	4	4	5	3	5	4	73-283
Joe Ogilvie USA £27,500	Round 1	4	4	4	3	3	4	5	3	3	4	4	3	4	4	4	5	4	4	69
	Round 2	3	4	3	4	3	5	4	4	2	4	4	3	3	4	5	4	5	4	68
	Round 3	4	4	5	3	3	4	5	5	3	4	4	3	3	4	4	4	4	5	71
	Round 4	3	4	4	5	4	5	5	4	3	3	4	4	4	4	7	4	4	4	75-283
Barry Lane England £25,000	Round 1	3	4	4	4	3	4	5	4	3	4	5	2	4	4	4	4	5	4	70
	Round 2	3	5	5	4	3	4	4	4	3	3	4	3	4	4	5	7	4	3	72
	Round 3	3	5	4	4	3	5	4	6	3	4	4	3	4	4	4	3	4	4	70-284
	Round 4	2	5	4	3	3	4	5	5	3	4	4	3	5	4	3	4	4	4	
Justin Rose England £21,500	Round 1	3	4	4	4	3	5	3	4	3	4	5	3	3	4	5	4	4	4	69
	Round 2	4	4	4	4	4	4	4	4	4	3	5	3	4	4	4	4	4	5	72
	Round 3	3	5	4	5	3	4	5	5	2	4	4	4	4	4	5	4	4	5	74
	Round 4	2	4	7	3	3	6	4	3	3	4	3	4	4	5	3	4	4	4	70-285
Stewart Cink USA £21,500	Round 1	3	5	3	4	3	4	6	3	2	4	4	3	4	4	6	4	5	4	71
	Round 2	3	4	4	4	3	5	5	4	3	4	4	4	4	3	5	3	5	4	72
	Round 3	4	3	4	4	4	5	4	4	2	4	5	3	4	4	3	4	4	5	70-285
	Round 4	3	4	4	3	3	5	5	4	2	4	5	3	4	3	4	4	5	5	
Phil Mickelson USA £21,500	Round 1	3	3	5	5	4	3	3	4	3	5	4	4	3	4	4	5	4	4	70
	Round 2	4	4	4	4	3	4	4	4	3	4	4	3	4	6	4	4	5	4	72
	Round 3	3	4	4	4	4	5	5	4	3	4	5	3	3	3	4	4	5	5	72
	Round 4	4	4	4	3	3	5	4	5	3	4	4	3	4	5	4	4	4	4	71-285

HOLE		1	2	3	4	5	6	7	8	9	10	11	12	13	14	15	16	17	18	TOTAL
PAR		3	4	4	4	3	5	5	4	3	4	5	3	4	4	4	4	4	4	
Phillip Price Wales £21,500	Round 1	3	4	4	3	3	5	6	4	3	4	4	4	5	4	6	4	4	4	74
	Round 2	4	4	3	4	3	4	6	4	2	4	5	3	3	4	3	4	5	4	69
	Round 3	3	5	6	4	3	4	4	4	2	4	5	3	3	4	4	4	5	4	71
	Round 4	3	4	5	5	3	4	4	3	2	3	7	3	4	4	4	5	4	4	71-285
Scott Verplank USA £21,500	Round 1	3	4	5	3	4	5	4	4	3	4	4	3	4	5	4	4	4	5	71
	Round 2	3	5	4	4	4	4	5	4	3	4	4	3	4	4	4	4	5	4	72
	Round 3	3	6	4	3	2	4	6	4	3	4	4	2	4	4	5	4	3	5	70
	Round 4	3	3	4	4	4	5	5	4	2	4	5	4	4	4	5	4	4	4	72-285
***David Dixon** England	Round 1	3	4	4	4	3	4	5	3	3	4	5	3	4	5	4	4	4	4	70
	Round 2	3	5	4	4	3	5	4	4	2	4	4	3	3	4	5	4	5	5	71
	Round 3	2	4	4	4	3	5	4	5	4	4	5	3	4	3	4	4	4	4	70
	Round 4	2	5	5	4	4	4	6	3	3	5	5	3	4	4	4	4	6	3	74-285
Nicolas Vanhootegem Belgium £21,500	Round 1	3	4	4	4	4	4	5	4	3	4	4	3	3	5	5	5	4	4	72
	Round 2	2	4	4	4	3	4	4	4	2	4	4	4	4	4	4	4	4	5	68
	Round 3	3	4	5	5	3	4	5	4	2	3	5	4	3	4	5	4	3	4	70
	Round 4	3	4	4	6	3	5	4	5	3	4	4	3	4	4	6	4	4	5	75-285
Padraig Harrington Ireland £16,300	Round 1	3	4	4	4	3	5	4	5	3	4	4	5	3	5	5	5	5	5	75
	Round 2	2	4	4	4	2	4	4	4	3	3	4	3	4	5	4	4	4	4	66
	Round 3	3	5	4	4	3	4	6	6	3	4	5	3	3	4	4	4	5	4	74
	Round 4	2	5	5	3	4	5	5	5	3	5	4	2	4	4	4	3	5	3	71-286
Frank Lickliter II USA £16,300	Round 1	3	4	5	4	3	6	3	4	3	4	6	3	3	5	4	4	4	3	71
	Round 2	3	4	6	5	1	4	5	3	3	4	5	4	4	4	4	4	4	4	71
	Round 3	3	4	6	4	3	4	4	5	2	4	6	3	4	4	5	4	4	4	73
	Round 4	2	3	4	4	4	4	5	4	3	5	6	3	4	4	4	4	4	4	71-286
Toru Taniguchi Japan £16,300	Round 1	3	4	4	4	3	4	4	5	4	4	5	3	4	4	4	4	4	5	72
	Round 2	3	4	5	4	3	4	4	4	3	3	5	3	4	4	4	4	4	4	69
	Round 3	3	4	5	4	3	5	4	4	3	4	5	3	3	4	4	4	6	4	72
	Round 4	4	4	5	5	3	4	5	4	3	4	5	3	4	4	3	4	4	5	73-286
Andrew Coltart Scotland £16,300	Round 1	3	4	4	5	4	4	8	5	3	4	5	3	4	4	4	4	3	4	75
	Round 2	4	3	4	4	3	5	4	3	3	4	5	3	4	4	3	4	5	3	68
	Round 3	3	5	5	4	3	4	4	5	3	4	5	3	3	3	4	4	4	4	70
	Round 4	3	5	4	4	3	4	5	3	3	4	5	4	5	4	3	4	5	5	73-286
Dudley Hart USA £16,300	Round 1	3	3	4	4	4	5	5	4	2	4	5	4	5	4	5	4	4	5	74
	Round 2	3	4	4	4	4	4	4	5	3	4	5	2	3	4	4	4	4	4	69
	Round 3	3	4	6	3	3	4	3	4	3	4	5	4	4	4	5	3	4	3	69
	Round 4	3	5	5	4	3	4	5	4	4	4	5	4	3	5	4	4	4	4	74-286
J.P. Hayes USA £13,500	Round 1	3	3	4	4	4	4	4	5	2	4	4	4	4	5	4	4	3		69
	Round 2	2	4	4	5	3	6	5	4	3	4	4	3	3	4	4	4	5	5	71
	Round 3	3	4	4	4	4	6	4	4	3	4	5	3	4	5	5	4	4		74
	Round 4	3	4	4	4	3	4	7	4	3	4	6	3	4	4	4	3	5	4	73-287
Richard Green Australia £13,500	Round 1	3	5	4	4	3	4	5	3	3	4	5	2	4	4	5	4	4	5	71
	Round 2	4	4	4	4	3	5	4	4	2	4	5	3	4	4	4	4	4	5	70
	Round 3	2	4	4	4	3	4	5	6	2	3	5	3	4	6	4	4	5	4	72
	Round 4	3	4	4	4	3	5	4	4	3	4	6	3	4	5	5	4	6	3	74-287
Steve Stricker USA £13,500	Round 1	3	3	3	5	4	5	5	4	3	4	5	3	4	3	4	4	5	4	71
	Round 2	3	4	5	5	2	4	5	4	2	4	5	3	3	4	4	4	4	4	69
	Round 3	3	4	4	4	5	6	5	4	3	4	4	3	4	4	4	4	4	3	72
	Round 4	3	4	4	4	3	5	5	4	3	5	5	4	4	4	4	4	4	6	75-287

HOLE		1	2	3	4	5	6	7	8	9	10	11	12	13	14	15	16	17	18	TOTAL
PAR		3	4	4	4	3	5	5	4	3	4	5	3	4	4	4	4	4	4	TOTAL
Mark O'Meara USA £13,500	Round 1	3	4	3	4	3	5	5	4	3	4	5	2	4	3	5	4	5	4	70
	Round 2	3	4	4	4	3	4	5	4	2	3	5	3	4	4	5	3	5	4	69
	Round 3	4	4	6	4	3	6	4	5	3	3	4	3	5	3	3	5	4	3	72
	Round 4	2	4	5	4	3	4	6	4	3	5	5	4	4	5	5	4	4	5	76-287
Paul Lawrie Scotland £13,500	Round 1	4	3	4	4	3	5	5	5	3	3	5	3	5	4	4	4	4	4	72
	Round 2	3	4	4	4	2	5	4	5	3	5	5	3	4	4	4	4	3	4	70
	Round 3	3	4	4	4	3	4	4	5	2	3	5	3	3	4	4	5	4	5	69
	Round 4	3	5	5	4	3	6	5	6	3	3	6	3	4	4	4	3	5	4	76-287
Peter Lonard Australia £10,629	Round 1	3	4	4	4	3	5	4	3	3	4	6	3	4	4	4	6	4	4	72
	Round 2	3	3	4	4	3	4	4	6	3	4	4	3	2	4	4	4	7	4	70
	Round 3	3	4	5	4	3	5	5	5	2	4	5	4	4	4	5	3	5	4	74
	Round 4	3	4	4	4	3	5	5	5	2	4	5	4	4	4	3	5	4	4	72-288
Robert Allenby Australia £10,629	Round 1	3	4	5	5	4	5	6	4	4	4	5	3	3	4	3	4	4	3	73
	Round 2	3	4	4	5	3	4	4	3	4	4	4	4	4	4	4	4	4	5	71
	Round 3	4	4	4	3	3	4	5	5	2	5	3	4	4	3	4	6	4	3	71
	Round 4	3	4	4	5	3	5	5	4	3	4	5	3	4	4	4	4	4	3	73-288
Chris DiMarco USA £10,629	Round 1	4	3	6	4	3	4	4	4	2	4	4	3	3	4	4	5	3	4	68
	Round 2	3	4	4	5	3	5	4	4	3	4	4	3	4	4	6	4	4	6	74
	Round 3	2	4	4	4	5	4	5	4	3	3	3	3	4	5	6	4	4	5	72
	Round 4	3	4	6	5	3	4	5	5	2	4	5	3	4	4	3	4	6	4	74-288
Lee Westwood England £10,629	Round 1	3	3	4	4	4	5	5	4	3	4	5	4	4	5	3	4	4	5	73
	Round 2	4	4	6	4	2	5	4	4	2	4	4	3	3	4	4	4	4	5	70
	Round 3	3	4	3	4	4	5	5	3	4	3	5	4	4	5	4	3	4	4	71
	Round 4	4	4	4	4	3	6	5	4	3	4	5	4	3	4	5	4	4	4	74-288
Matt Gogel USA £10,629	Round 1	4	3	4	5	2	4	6	5	4	4	4	3	4	5	4	4	4	4	73
	Round 2	3	4	4	4	3	3	5	4	3	3	5	4	4	4	4	3	4	6	70
	Round 3	3	3	5	5	3	5	4	5	3	3	4	3	4	4	4	4	4	5	71
	Round 4	4	4	5	4	3	5	5	4	3	4	5	3	4	4	5	4	4	4	74-288
Adam Scott Australia £10,629	Round 1	3	4	4	3	4	5	4	4	3	4	5	4	4	5	4	4	5	4	73
	Round 2	3	5	4	5	3	4	4	4	3	3	4	3	4	6	4	4	5	3	71
	Round 3	3	4	4	5	3	4	5	4	3	3	4	4	3	5	5	3	4	4	70
	Round 4	3	3	4	4	4	4	6	4	2	4	5	5	4	4	4	5	5	4	74-288
Brad Faxon USA £10,629	Round 1	3	3	5	4	3	3	4	3	4	4	4	4	4	4	4	4	3	5	68
	Round 2	3	3	4	4	3	6	4	5	4	4	5	3	4	4	3	4	5	3	71
	Round 3	4	4	4	5	3	5	4	4	3	5	5	3	4	4	4	4	7	3	74
	Round 4	3	4	5	4	4	5	4	4	3	5	5	3	4	4	4	4	7	3	75-288
Jose Maria Olazabal Spain £8,943	Round 1	3	3	4	4	3	4	5	3	3	4	4	4	4	5	4	4	4	4	69
	Round 2	3	5	5	5	3	4	4	5	3	4	5	3	4	4	4	4	5	4	74
	Round 3	3	4	4	4	3	4	5	5	3	4	6	3	4	4	3	5	5	4	73
	Round 4	3	4	3	3	4	5	7	4	3	4	5	3	4	5	4	3	5	4	73-289
Rory Sabbatini South Africa £8,943	Round 1	3	3	4	4	3	5	4	4	3	4	5	4	3	6	4	3	4	4	70
	Round 2	2	5	4	5	3	4	5	4	4	2	3	4	3	4	5	4	4	4	69
	Round 3	3	4	5	5	3	4	5	4	3	4	6	4	4	4	7	3	4	4	76
	Round 4	3	4	6	3	4	4	5	4	4	3	4	5	4	4	4	4	5	3	74-289
Carlos Franco Paraguay £8,943	Round 1	3	4	4	3	3	4	5	4	3	5	5	4	3	5	4	4	4	4	71
	Round 2	3	4	5	5	3	4	4	4	3	4	4	2	4	4	5	4	5	4	71
	Round 3	3	5	4	4	3	3	4	4	3	4	4	3	4	4	5	4	5	6	73
	Round 4	2	5	5	4	3	4	5	5	3	4	6	2	4	3	5	4	5	5	74-289

HOLE		1	2	3	4	5	6	7	8	9	10	11	12	13	14	15	16	17	18	
PAR		3	4	4	4	3	5	5	4	3	4	5	3	4	4	4	4	4	4	TOTAL
Mark Calcavecchia	Round 1	3	4	4	4	4	4	5	5	3	4	5	3	4	5	4	3	4	4	72
USA	Round 2	3	4	7	4	3	4	4	4	3	4	4	3	5	3	4	3	4	4	70
£8,943	Round 3	3	3	4	4	4	5	4	4	3	4	5	3	4	4	4	4	4	6	72
	Round 4	3	4	6	4	4	5	4	5	2	4	5	3	5	3	5	4	4	5	75-289
Paul Curry	Round 1	3	5	4	4	3	4	4	4	3	4	6	3	3	5	4	5	4	4	72
England	Round 2	3	4	5	4	3	5	4	4	3	4	5	3	4	4	4	4	4	4	71
£8,943	Round 3	3	4	4	4	3	5	5	4	3	4	5	3	4	4	4	4	4	4	71
	Round 4	3	4	4	4	3	5	5	5	3	4	5	3	5	4	4	4	6	4	75-289
Paul McGinley	Round 1	2	4	5	4	3	4	5	5	3	3	4	3	3	5	5	3	4	4	69
Ireland	Round 2	3	4	5	4	3	4	4	4	3	4	4	3	4	4	5	5	5	4	72
£8,943	Round 3	2	4	5	5	2	4	5	3	3	4	4	3	4	4	5	4	5	6	72
	Round 4	3	4	4	4	3	5	5	5	3	4	5	4	4	4	6	4	4	5	76-289
Duffy Waldorf	Round 1	3	3	5	4	3	6	4	3	3	4	4	2	4	4	5	4	5	4	70
USA	Round 2	4	4	5	4	3	4	4	5	3	4	4	3	4	4	4	4	5	5	73
£8,943	Round 3	3	4	4	4	3	4	4	4	3	4	5	3	3	4	5	4	3	5	69
	Round 4	4	4	4	5	3	7	4	4	4	3	6	4	3	4	5	4	4	5	77-289
Stuart Appleby	Round 1	3	4	4	4	3	4	4	5	2	4	6	3	4	4	4	4	3	4	69
Australia	Round 2	3	5	7	4	4	5	4	4	3	3	5	3	4	4	4	4	4	5	75
£8,500	Round 3	3	4	5	5	3	5	4	4	4	3	4	3	3	5	4	4	5	4	72
	Round 4	3	5	4	5	4	5	6	4	4	3	5	4	4	4	4	3	3	4	74-290
Gordon Brand Jnr	Round 1	3	4	5	4	3	4	5	4	3	4	5	4	4	4	4	3	3	4	70
Scotland	Round 2	4	5	3	5	3	5	5	4	3	4	4	4	4	4	4	3	4	4	72
£8,400	Round 3	3	4	5	5	3	5	4	5	3	4	5	3	4	4	5	4	4	5	75
	Round 4	2	4	4	4	3	5	5	5	3	5	4	3	5	4	5	5	4	4	74-291
Brandel Chamblee	Round 1	4	5	4	4	3	5	4	3	4	4	4	3	4	4	4	4	5	4	72
USA	Round 2	3	4	4	4	3	4	5	4	3	4	5	4	3	5	4	3	3	4	69
£8,400	Round 3	4	4	4	4	4	5	5	4	3	5	4	3	3	4	4	4	5	5	74
	Round 4	3	4	5	5	4	5	5	5	3	4	5	3	4	4	4	4	4	5	76-291
Pierre Fulke	Round 1	3	4	4	4	2	4	5	3	3	4	4	3	5	4	4	4	5	4	69
Sweden	Round 2	3	4	4	4	3	4	4	4	3	3	4	3	4	4	4	4	4	4	67
£8,400	Round 3	3	3	4	4	3	5	6	4	4	4	5	3	4	3	6	4	4	3	72
	Round 4	4	5	5	5	3	5	5	4	3	4	6	8	4	4	5	4	6	3	83-291
Neil Cheetham	Round 1	3	4	4	5	4	5	5	4	4	4	4	4	3	4	3	4	4	4	72
England	Round 2	3	4	4	4	4	5	4	4	3	4	5	2	4	4	5	4	5	4	72
£8,300	Round 3	3	5	3	5	3	4	4	4	3	3	6	3	4	5	4	4	5	5	73
	Round 4	2	6	5	5	4	4	4	4	3	3	7	3	4	5	6	4	5	4	78-295
Thomas Levet	Round 1	4	4	5	4	3	5	5	3	4	4	4	3	4	4	4	3	4	5	72
France	Round 2	3	4	6	4	3	4	5	4	3	4	5	3	4	5	3	4	4	4	72
£8,225	Round 3	4	3	5	3	4	3	7	5	3	4	5	3	5	5	5	4	5	4	77
	Round 4	3	4	4	4	3	5	8	4	3	6	3	3	4	3	5	4	4	5	75-296
Alexandre Balicki	Round 1	3	4	4	4	3	4	5	4	3	3	5	3	5	4	3	4	4	4	69
France	Round 2	3	5	4	4	2	6	6	4	3	4	5	3	4	4	3	5	5	4	75
£8,225	Round 3	3	4	4	4	3	5	5	4	3	3	5	3	4	6	5	5	5	5	75
	Round 4	2	4	4	4	3	6	5	5	3	5	4	4	4	5	5	5	4	5	77-296
David Smail	Round 1	4	4	4	4	3	5	5	3	3	3	5	4	4	4	5	3	4	4	71
New Zealand	Round 2	3	4	4	5	3	5	6	4	3	5	5	3	3	3	4	3	4	5	72
£8,150	Round 3	4	4	5	4	4	4	4	4	3	5	5	4	4	5	5	4	5	4	76
	Round 4	4	4	5	4	3	6	4	3	3	5	6	3	4	5	5	6	4	5	79-298

HOLE		1	2	3	4	5	6	7	8	9	10	11	12	13	14	15	16	17	18	
PAR		3	4	4	4	3	5	5	4	3	4	5	3	4	4	4	4	4	4	TOTAL
Scott Henderson	Round 1	3	3	5	5	4	4	4	4	3	5	4	4	4	6	4	4	5		75
Scotland	Round 2	3	4	5	5	3	5	4	4	2	3	4	4	4	4	4	4	3		69
£8,075	Round 3	3	5	6	5	3	7	5	4	4	5	5	2	4	5	5	4	5	4	81
	Round 4	3	4	4	6	3	6	5	4	3	4	5	3	4	5	3	5	5		76-301
Sandy Lyle	Round 1	3	4	4	4	2	5	3	5	3	4	4	4	5	4	4	4	6		72
Scotland	Round 2	3	4	4	3	4	4	4	5	3	3	4	4	5	5	4	4	4		71
£8,075	Round 3	2	4	5	3	4	4	4	5	3	6	3	4	4	4	4	4	6		77
	Round 4	4	4	6	3	4	5	4	5	3	4	6	3	4	6	6	4	5	4	81-301

NON QUALIFIERS AFTER 36 HOLES

(Leading 10 professionals and ties receive £1,300 each, next 20 professionals and ties receive £1,100 each, next 20 professionals and ties receive £1,000 each, remainder of professionals receive £900 each.)

HOLE		1	2	3	4	5	6	7	8	9	10	11	12	13	14	15	16	17	18	
PAR		3	4	4	4	3	5	5	4	3	4	5	3	4	4	4	4	4	4	TOTAL
John Bickerton	Round 1	3	3	5	5	4	4	6	4	4	4	4	3	3	6	4	3	4	5	74
England	Round 2	3	4	5	3	3	5	5	4	2	4	5	4	4	4	4	4	4	4	71-145
Mathias Gronberg	Round 1	3	5	4	4	4	5	4	5	3	4	5	4	2	5	5	4	4	5	75
Sweden	Round 2	3	4	4	4	3	5	5	3	3	5	5	4	4	4	3	3	4	4	70-145
Soren Kjeldsen	Round 1	4	4	4	4	2	5	5	3	3	4	4	4	4	5	5	4	5	4	73
Denmark	Round 2	3	4	5	3	3	4	5	4	3	4	6	3	4	4	5	3	4	5	72-145
Jean Hugo	Round 1	3	4	3	4	4	4	5	4	3	5	4	4	5	3	5	5	4	4	73
South Africa	Round 2	4	4	6	4	2	4	3	4	3	5	4	3	5	4	4	4	4	5	72-145
Joe Durant	Round 1	3	4	5	4	4	4	6	4	4	4	5	3	4	4	4	4	5	4	75
USA	Round 2	4	3	4	5	3	5	5	3	3	3	4	3	4	3	4	4	4	6	70-145
Justin Leonard	Round 1	3	3	5	5	3	3	5	5	3	4	5	4	3	5	4	5	5	4	74
USA	Round 2	3	3	4	4	3	5	5	4	3	4	4	3	4	5	5	4	5	4	71-145
Steve Flesch	Round 1	3	4	4	4	3	4	4	3	4	4	6	4	3	5	6	4	5	4	74
USA	Round 2	4	4	4	4	2	4	6	4	3	4	5	3	5	5	3	4	4	3	71-145
Peter O'Malley	Round 1	2	3	7	4	3	5	5	4	3	4	5	3	3	4	4	4	5	3	71
Australia	Round 2	3	3	4	5	3	5	4	4	4	6	5	3	4	4	4	4	5	4	74-145
Stephen Leaney	Round 1	3	4	4	5	4	5	5	4	2	4	4	5	4	5	6	4	4	4	76
Australia	Round 2	3	4	4	3	3	4	5	5	2	3	5	3	4	4	4	4	5	4	69-145
Fredrik Jacobson	Round 1	3	4	4	4	2	5	8	4	4	4	5	4	4	4	4	4	4	4	74
Sweden	Round 2	4	4	4	4	3	5	5	4	2	4	4	3	4	3	4	4	5	5	71-145
Gary Birch	Round 1	3	4	5	3	2	5	9	4	4	4	5	4	3	4	4	4	4	4	75
Germany	Round 2	4	4	4	4	3	4	3	4	3	4	4	3	4	5	5	4	4	4	70-145
Markus Brier	Round 1	3	4	6	3	4	5	5	4	3	4	6	3	4	3	5	4	5	3	74
Austria	Round 2	4	4	4	5	3	4	4	5	2	4	5	2	4	4	4	4	5	4	71-145
Taichi Teshima	Round 1	3	4	5	4	4	5	4	4	3	4	4	4	4	5	4	4	4	5	74
Japan	Round 2	4	4	5	4	3	4	5	4	2	4	5	4	4	4	3	4	4	5	72-146
Nick Faldo	Round 1	3	4	4	4	2	4	4	6	4	5	6	3	4	4	5	4	4	5	75
England	Round 2	3	4	3	5	4	5	4	4	3	4	5	3	4	4	4	4	4	4	71-146
Mark Brooks	Round 1	3	6	4	4	4	5	6	4	3	4	4	2	4	4	4	4	4	4	73
USA	Round 2	3	5	4	4	3	6	5	4	3	3	5	3	4	4	4	3	5	5	73-146
Robert Karlsson	Round 1	3	6	5	4	2	5	5	4	3	4	5	3	4	4	5	4	4	5	75
Sweden	Round 2	3	4	4	4	4	5	5	3	4	4	5	3	4	3	4	3	4	5	71-146
Corey Pavin	Round 1	3	4	4	4	3	5	6	4	3	3	4	3	5	5	4	3	4	4	71
USA	Round 2	3	4	5	4	3	4	5	3	3	4	6	4	4	4	5	4	4	6	75-146
Bradford Vaughan	Round 1	4	4	4	4	2	5	5	3	3	4	5	3	4	4	4	4	4	4	72
South Africa	Round 2	3	5	4	3	4	5	4	5	3	4	5	4	4	4	4	5	4	5	74-146
Soren Hansen	Round 1	3	4	6	4	3	4	4	4	3	5	5	3	4	4	4	4	4	3	71
Denmark	Round 2	4	6	5	3	3	4	5	4	3	3	6	3	4	4	4	5	4	5	75-146
Matthew Cort	Round 1	3	4	5	4	4	5	5	4	3	4	5	4	4	5	5	4	4	5	77
England	Round 2	3	4	4	3	3	5	5	4	3	4	4	3	3	5	4	4	4	4	69-146
Roberts Coles	Round 1	3	4	4	4	4	5	4	4	3	4	5	3	4	5	5	4	4	4	73
England	Round 2	3	4	4	4	3	5	4	4	3	4	5	3	4	4	4	4	6	5	73-146

HOLE		1	2	3	4	5	6	7	8	9	10	11	12	13	14	15	16	17	18	TOTAL
PAR		3	4	4	4	3	5	5	4	3	4	5	3	4	4	4	4	4	4	
Shigeki Maruyama (Japan)	Round 1	2	4	4	4	2	5	7	5	5	3	5	4	4	5	4	4	3	5	75
	Round 2	3	4	5	4	3	4	5	4	3	5	5	3	3	4	4	5	4	3	71-146
Dinesh Chand (Fiji)	Round 1	3	4	4	5	3	5	4	4	4	4	5	4	3	4	5	4	4	6	75
	Round 2	4	5	3	3	3	5	6	3	3	3	4	3	4	4	6	4	4	4	71-146
Scott Hoch (USA)	Round 1	3	4	4	5	3	5	6	4	4	4	5	3	4	5	4	4	4	4	75
	Round 2	4	4	4	5	2	5	4	4	3	4	4	3	4	4	5	4	5	4	72-147
Tom Lehman (USA)	Round 1	3	5	5	4	3	5	5	5	2	5	5	2	4	5	5	4	4	4	75
	Round 2	2	4	5	4	3	6	5	4	3	3	4	3	4	3	5	4	4	6	72-147
Aaron Baddeley (Australia)	Round 1	4	4	4	5	3	5	5	5	3	4	4	3	4	4	5	4	4	5	75
	Round 2	3	4	5	5	3	5	5	3	2	3	4	4	5	4	4	5	4	4	72-147
*Stuart Wilson (Scotland)	Round 1	3	5	3	5	4	5	4	4	4	4	7	4	4	5	4	4	4	4	77
	Round 2	2	3	5	4	3	5	4	5	3	4	4	3	4	4	5	4	4	4	70-147
David Howell (England)	Round 1	3	4	4	4	3	4	6	3	3	4	6	3	4	5	4	5	4	5	74
	Round 2	3	3	4	4	4	5	5	4	3	4	5	3	4	4	4	4	5	5	73-147
David Toms (USA)	Round 1	3	5	6	4	4	4	5	4	2	4	7	3	3	5	4	3	4	4	74
	Round 2	3	4	4	6	3	4	6	4	3	3	5	3	3	4	4	4	6	4	73-147
Olle Karlsson (Sweden)	Round 1	3	4	5	4	4	4	4	5	4	4	5	3	4	4	4	4	3	4	72
	Round 2	3	5	4	3	4	4	7	3	3	3	4	3	4	5	7	4	4	5	75-147
Mark Wiebe (USA)	Round 1	3	5	4	4	3	5	4	3	2	4	6	3	4	5	5	5	4	4	73
	Round 2	3	4	4	4	3	4	4	4	3	4	7	3	4	4	5	4	5	5	74-147
Mark Pilkington (Wales)	Round 1	3	4	5	4	3	6	5	6	3	5	5	2	4	4	4	4	3	3	77
	Round 2	3	4	5	5	3	5	5	4	3	4	4	3	4	4	4	4	3	3	70-147
John Daly (USA)	Round 1	3	4	6	3	4	4	4	4	4	4	4	3	3	4	5	5	4	4	72
	Round 2	3	4	5	6	3	5	5	6	3	6	5	2	3	4	5	3	4	4	76-148
Jose Coceres (Argentina)	Round 1	3	5	4	4	3	4	5	3	3	4	4	3	4	4	6	4	4	4	71
	Round 2	3	4	6	4	3	5	4	6	2	4	4	3	5	4	6	5	5	4	77-148
Gary Orr (Scotland)	Round 1	3	5	4	3	3	5	4	4	3	4	5	3	5	4	5	5	3	5	73
	Round 2	3	4	4	5	3	5	5	5	3	5	7	3	3	4	4	4	4	4	75-148
Jeff Maggert (USA)	Round 1	3	3	4	4	3	2	6	4	3	4	5	3	6	3	5	6	4	4	72
	Round 2	3	4	7	4	3	4	5	4	3	4	5	3	4	4	7	4	4	4	76-148
Dennis Paulson (USA)	Round 1	3	4	5	5	4	4	6	5	3	5	6	3	4	4	5	4	4	4	78
	Round 2	3	4	4	5	3	4	4	5	3	3	6	3	4	4	4	3	4	4	70-148
David Frost (South Africa)	Round 1	3	4	6	4	4	4	5	4	2	3	5	4	5	5	5	3	4	4	74
	Round 2	4	4	5	4	3	5	5	3	3	3	5	3	4	4	7	4	4	4	74-148
Brian Gay (USA)	Round 1	3	4	5	5	3	4	4	5	3	4	5	4	3	5	4	4	4	3	72
	Round 2	4	4	5	4	3	6	4	4	3	4	6	3	4	4	4	5	5	4	76-148
Daren Lee (England)	Round 1	3	5	4	3	4	5	4	4	2	3	4	5	3	5	8	4	5	5	76
	Round 2	3	4	4	4	4	5	4	5	2	4	4	4	4	4	4	4	5	4	72-148
Nobuhito Sato (Japan)	Round 1	2	6	4	5	3	4	7	6	3	4	6	4	4	4	4	3	4	3	76
	Round 2	4	4	3	4	3	4	4	4	3	4	3	3	4	4	5	4	5	6	72-148
*Jeff Quinney (USA)	Round 1	3	4	4	4	3	5	5	5	4	4	5	6	4	3	5	4	5	5	76
	Round 2	3	4	5	5	3	4	5	4	3	5	4	3	4	3	5	4	5	4	73-149
Andrew Oldcorn (Scotland)	Round 1	3	4	4	5	4	4	5	3	3	4	5	3	4	4	6	3	4	5	73
	Round 2	4	5	4	4	3	4	5	5	3	4	6	3	4	5	4	4	5	4	76-149
Bob May (USA)	Round 1	3	4	4	4	3	4	4	4	3	5	6	3	5	5	5	4	6	5	77
	Round 2	3	4	5	4	3	4	5	5	4	3	5	3	4	5	3	4	4	4	72-149

HOLE		1	2	3	4	5	6	7	8	9	10	11	12	13	14	15	16	17	18	
PAR		3	4	4	4	3	5	5	4	3	4	5	3	4	4	4	4	4	4	TOTAL
Mark McNulty	Round 1	2	4	4	4	4	5	5	3	3	4	5	3	4	3	4	5	4	4	70
Zimbabwe	Round 2	3	4	4	4	3	5	5	4	3	4	5	3	5	5	4	4	7	7	79-149
Seve Ballesteros	Round 1	3	4	4	5	4	5	5	4	4	4	4	4	5	5	5	4	5	5	78
Spain	Round 2	3	4	5	5	2	4	4	4	4	4	5	3	4	3	4	4	5	4	71-149
Bob Charles	Round 1	3	4	5	4	3	4	4	5	3	4	5	3	5	4	5	4	5	5	75
New Zealand	Round 2	2	5	4	4	5	6	5	4	3	4	5	4	3	4	3	4	5	4	74-149
Tony Jacklin	Round 1	3	4	4	3	5	5	5	5	3	4	5	4	3	5	4	5	4	4	75
England	Round 2	3	3	5	4	4	5	5	4	2	4	5	3	4	5	5	5	4	4	74-149
***Michael Hoey**	Round 1	3	4	4	4	4	5	5	4	3	4	4	4	4	5	4	5	4	3	73
N. Ireland	Round 2	3	4	4	4	4	7	6	4	3	3	4	3	4	4	6	4	5	4	76-149
Steve Elkington	Round 1	3	5	4	5	4	4	4	4	3	4	5	4	6	4	5	4	5	4	77
Australia	Round 2	4	4	4	4	2	5	5	4	2	4	6	3	4	5	5	3	4	4	72-149
Fred Couples	Round 1	3	4	5	4	4	4	3	4	2	4	5	2	4	7	4	4	4	4	71
USA	Round 2	4	5	5	5	3	6	5	4	4	5	5	4	4	3	5	4	3	4	78-149
Carl Paulson	Round 1	3	4	4	4	3	5	4	6	3	3	5	3	4	4	4	4	4	5	72
USA	Round 2	3	5	5	4	4	4	8	4	2	4	4	3	4	4	6	4	5	4	77-149
Mike Weir	Round 1	3	4	5	4	3	5	5	4	3	4	4	3	6	5	5	4	5	6	78
Canada	Round 2	4	5	6	4	3	5	4	3	2	4	4	3	3	6	4	3	4	5	72-150
Naomichi Ozaki	Round 1	3	5	3	4	3	4	6	4	3	4	3	4	6	5	5	4	5	5	77
Japan	Round 2	6	4	4	4	3	5	7	4	2	4	4	3	3	4	4	3	4	5	73-150
***Matthew Griffiths**	Round 1	3	4	4	4	3	5	4	4	3	4	5	3	4	4	5	3	5	6	73
Wales	Round 2	4	4	5	5	4	5	6	4	3	5	5	3	4	4	4	4	4	4	77-150
Nathan Green	Round 1	3	4	4	4	3	4	5	4	2	4	6	3	5	6	4	4	5	5	75
Australia	Round 2	3	4	4	4	3	5	4	4	3	4	4	4	4	6	4	4	4	7	75-150
Simon Dyson	Round 1	3	4	6	5	3	5	5	5	3	4	5	3	4	5	5	4	5	3	77
England	Round 2	3	5	6	4	4	4	4	4	3	4	5	3	5	5	5	4	4	3	73-150
Shingo Katayama	Round 1	4	4	5	4	3	4	5	4	2	5	6	4	4	5	4	5	4	3	75
Japan	Round 2	3	4	6	4	3	4	6	5	3	4	5	2	4	4	4	4	4	6	75-150
Dean Wilson	Round 1	3	4	4	4	3	5	5	4	3	4	5	2	4	4	4	5	5	4	72
USA	Round 2	3	5	4	4	3	5	9	5	4	3	4	2	4	4	4	5	5	5	78-150
Jerry Kelly	Round 1	3	4	4	5	3	4	5	5	3	5	5	4	3	4	4	5	4	4	74
USA	Round 2	3	4	5	5	3	5	4	4	3	5	4	3	6	4	6	4	5	4	77-151
Steve Jones	Round 1	3	5	4	4	3	5	4	4	3	5	5	3	4	4	5	4	4	5	74
USA	Round 2	4	4	5	5	3	4	7	5	4	4	4	4	4	4	4	4	4	4	77-151
Mark Roe	Round 1	3	4	4	4	4	5	4	4	3	5	6	3	4	4	4	4	4	4	73
England	Round 2	4	5	6	4	4	4	4	4	2	4	4	3	4	4	6	6	5	5	78-151
Thomas Bjorn	Round 1	3	3	6	4	3	4	8	4	3	4	5	4	3	5	4	4	4	5	76
Denmark	Round 2	2	4	4	6	4	4	4	5	3	4	7	3	3	5	5	3	4	4	75-151
John Huston	Round 1	3	5	6	4	4	5	5	5	3	4	5	4	4	4	4	4	5	4	76
USA	Round 2	3	5	6	3	3	6	5	5	2	4	4	4	4	4	4	4	5	4	75-151
Brett Rumford	Round 1	3	3	5	4	3	4	9	4	3	4	4	3	4	4	4	4	4	4	73
Australia	Round 2	3	4	4	5	3	4	4	4	3	5	8	3	4	5	5	6	4	4	78-151
Geoff Ogilvy	Round 1	3	4	4	4	3	5	5	5	3	4	6	3	4	5	5	5	4	4	76
Australia	Round 2	3	7	5	4	3	5	5	3	4	4	4	3	4	5	5	3	4	4	75-151
Jean Van de Velde	Round 1	5	5	6	3	4	4	4	4	4	4	5	3	4	4	5	4	5	4	77
France	Round 2	4	5	4	4	3	4	6	3	3	4	5	4	4	4	5	4	5	4	75-152

HOLE		1	2	3	4	5	6	7	8	9	10	11	12	13	14	15	16	17	18	TOTAL
PAR		3	4	4	4	3	5	5	4	3	4	5	3	4	4	4	4	4	4	
Tom Watson	Round 1	3	5	5	4	4	5	4	4	3	4	6	3	4	4	4	3	3	6	74
USA	Round 2	3	4	5	4	3	6	4	4	5	4	6	4	4	4	3	6	5		78-152
Henrik Stenson	Round 1	4	4	5	4	4	5	5	4	3	4	5	3	5	4	4	4	4	4	75
Sweden	Round 2	3	4	5	6	3	7	4	4	4	4	5	3	4	4	5	4	4	4	77-152
Roger Chapman	Round 1	3	4	4	4	4	5	5	5	3	4	6	3	4	4	5	5	5	3	76
England	Round 2	4	5	4	4	3	4	5	3	7	4	3	4	4	4	6	4	4	4	76-152
Jim Furyk	Round 1	3	5	4	4	3	4	4	4	3	3	10	4	5	4	5	4	4	4	77
USA	Round 2	3	4	4	4	3	5	5	4	3	4	5	2	4	4	7	4	4	6	75-152
Greg Turner	Round 1	4	3	5	4	3	5	5	5	3	4	6	4	4	5	5	4	5	5	79
New Zealand	Round 2	3	3	6	4	4	4	4	5	3	6	4	5	3	4	3	3	5	4	73-152
Mark Sanders	Round 1	4	3	4	5	4	6	6	4	4	5	7	4	3	5	4	4	4	3	79
England	Round 2	5	4	4	3	3	5	4	4	4	3	5	3	4	4	6	3	5	4	73-152
Juan Carlos Aguero	Round 1	4	4	4	4	3	4	5	5	3	5	5	3	3	5	4	5	6	5	77
Spain	Round 2	4	4	5	4	3	5	5	5	3	5	4	4	4	5	4	4	4	5	76-154
Hidemichi Tanaka	Round 1	4	4	4	5	3	5	5	4	2	5	4	3	4	4	5	6	5	4	76
Japan	Round 2	3	4	5	5	3	5	5	4	3	4	6	3	4	4	6	5	5	4	78-154
***John Kemp**	Round 1	3	5	4	4	4	4	5	4	4	6	6	3	4	5	4	4	4	3	76
England	Round 2	3	4	4	4	3	5	5	4	3	4	6	3	4	4	7	5	5	5	78-154
Graham Rankin	Round 1	3	4	5	4	4	4	5	4	3	5	5	3	4	5	6	5	6	4	79
Scotland	Round 2	4	4	6	5	3	5	5	3	3	4	5	3	4	4	4	3	5	5	75-154
Angel Cabrera	Round 1	3	4	6	5	4	5	6	5	5	4	5	3	4	5	4	4	6	4	80
Argentina	Round 2	3	3	4	4	3	6	6	4	4	4	4	4	3	5	4	4	4	4	75-155
Wayne Riley	Round 1	4	4	5	4	4	5	5	4	6	4	6	4	3	4	4	4	4	4	78
Australia	Round 2	3	4	4	5	3	5	4	4	2	4	5	4	3	5	6	6	5	5	77-155
Toshiaki Odate	Round 1	4	3	4	4	3	6	4	4	3	4	5	4	6	5	5	3	4	5	76
Japan	Round 2	4	5	3	6	3	4	4	5	3	4	4	4	5	5	4	4	8	5	80-156
Matthew McGuire	Round 1	3	4	3	5	3	4	4	4	3	3	5	4	4	5	4	4	3	6	71
England	Round 2	3	3	5	6	6	7	4	9	4	3	5	4	3	5	4	4	5	5	85-156
Simon Vale	Round 1	3	3	6	5	3	4	7	4	4	5	7	4	5	5	6	5	5	4	85
England	Round 2	3	4	5	5	3	5	4	5	2	3	5	4	4	3	5	5	4	5	74-159
Gary Player	Round 1	5	4	5	5	3	5	5	4	3	5	5	3	4	5	4	4	4	4	77
South Africa	Round 2	3	4	6	6	3	5	5	5	3	4	6	4	3	5	5	4	6	5	82-159
Stuart Callen	Round 1	3	5	4	5	3	4	7	3	4	4	6	3	2	5	4	4	7	5	78
Scotland	Round 2	3	5	5	4	3	5	7	4	2	4	8	4	5	6	4	5	5	3	82-160
Rocco Mediate	Round 1	3	4	6	4	4	4	4	4	2	4	5	3	4	5	4	5	4	5	74-WD
USA																				
Chris Perry	Round 1	3	3	4	4	4	6	5	5	3	4	4	5	5	5	5	4	4	5	78-WD
USA																				

ROYAL LYTHAM AND ST.ANNE'S GOLF CLUB